Raising a
Moral Child

RAISING A MORAL CHILD

How Faith Shapes Behavior

Jeanne
Hunt

Paulist Press
New York / Mahwah, NJ

Cover images all from Shutterstock.com. Photographer/copyright, clockwise from top left: Hurst Photo, Gelpi JM, Pressmaster, Blend Images. Cover and book design by Sharyn Banks

Library of Congress Cataloging-in-Publication Data

Hunt, Jeanne.
    Raising a moral child : how faith shapes behavior / Jeanne Hunt.
        pages cm
    ISBN 978-0-8091-4861-5 (alk. paper) — ISBN 978-1-58768-351-0
    1. Parenting—Religious aspects—Catholic Church. 2. Child rearing—Religious aspects—Catholic Church. 3. Children—Conduct of life. I. Title.
    BX2352.H85 2014
    248.8`45—dc23

                                                                    2013043243

ISBN 978-0-8091-4861-5 (paperback)
ISBN 978-1-58768-351-0 (e-book)

Published by Paulist Press
997 Macarthur Boulevard
Mahwah, New Jersey 07430

www.paulistpress.com

Printed and bound in the
United States of America

For Dottie and Stan, my parents,
who taught their children well

Contents

Introduction

From observation and interaction with thousands of parents, I have learned that many parents have lost touch with—or sadly, don't even know—the simple, commonsense methods of raising children who know the difference between right and wrong and are encouraged to live lives that are "good, right, and perfect." For that reason, I wrote *Raising a Moral Child* for everyone who plays a part in the moral formation of a child: parents, teachers, coaches, mentors, family members. My intent in detailing how faith shapes behavior is to give you encouragement and a firm prod to pass down to those who come after you the wisdom you have received and now want to give your own children.

The book is filled with homespun wisdom, not the stuff of psychologists or counselors, although much of the advice here can be found in professional journals if you really want to poke around. I don't cite statistics and studies, just real stories and tried-and-tested suggestions for teaching a child how to do the right thing. The stories you will encounter are real. Only the names have been changed to protect parents from their children.

My primary expertise is as a mother of four who has fought—and continues to fight—the good fight of forming moral children. So much of what I say comes from those years of holding the line of moral good in my own family. And too, as a lay pastoral minister in the Catholic church, I have worked for years in the arenas of parish and school, counseled hundreds of families, and prayed my heart out for all of us who find ourselves confronted on all sides by a world that disregards the call to live moral lives.

Raising a Moral Child can become a go-to resource to support you in your role as a shaper of children's character. Throughout the nine chapters you will encounter practical ways to implement abstract theory. At the end of each chapter, you will find tools for integrating the chapter's theme: questions to ponder, an easy exercise to put into practice what you've just read, and a prayer to focus your soul on the task of setting the moral direction for your child. The book can be used by individuals and by any group that wants to address together the challenges of raising a moral child. I encourage groups of parents to band together to flesh out your responses to the issues. There is safety and much wisdom in numbers!

I offer a word of encouragement and hope to all of you who think it is too late to change your lives or feel overwhelmed

by the task ahead: God only asks that you do your best to follow his ways. *Raising a Moral Child* is simply one way to hold
another's hand along the journey of discipleship. Take my hand,
and we will walk these pages together toward goodness and
trust in God's care.

CHAPTER 1

Morality Is a Learned Behavior

Recently, in a supermarket parking lot, I overheard a conversation between a mother and her son as they headed to their car. Apparently, the little boy had witnessed a cashier being rude to an elderly lady. The mother wanted her son to know that what the cashier had done was wrong. When the little boy asked his mother how he would know when something he did was wrong, the mother said, "Well, you know, just do what's 'appropriate.'" The little boy asked, "What does 'appropriate' mean?" The mother could not answer him. She seemed to have no idea how to teach her son what makes something wrong.

In my many years of teaching and speaking to groups about the faith formation of children, one thing has remained constant: parents, grandparents, teachers, and even civic authorities are worried about our children who seem to have little or no idea about what makes a behavior wrong or right. During nearly every diocesan workshop or parents' night in a parish where I have shared practical tips for raising a moral child, the audience is almost unanimous in telling me that children today have no idea what truly makes something wrong.

Statistics back this up: in a recent poll of children aged thirteen, the majority of young people believe that what makes something wrong is "getting caught." This finding alone gives great cause for worry because it is evidence that the moral lessons needed to learn right and wrong are not being taught. There is more—so much more—to living a moral life than not getting caught.

In our time, there is an impetus to reconnect with God. It seems that parents and educators alike sense that something has been missing. Perhaps the very cause of our children's lack of understanding of what is wrong and right is the lack of knowing a loving and merciful Divine Parent. As we begin to share that discovery with our children, I believe that the lost sense of knowing what is good, right, and perfect will return. There is an added bonus to teaching our children to have a relationship with this merciful God: we will learn again what we have forgotten. God is the source of all goodness and grace. God eagerly awaits leading all of us into wisdom and peace.

Our secular culture has long since lost track of moral right and wrong. In fact, those who stand up for morality are often ridiculed as prudish and out of touch. The mantra of our world is that if it pleases you, it is good. It is the task of parents, grandparents, teachers, and even civil authorities to return to the work of forming moral children. What we have lost, we must rediscover.

WITNESS WHAT WE BELIEVE

Moral lessons must first be taught at home. The great solution to teaching wrong from right is so simple that we miss it: we cannot preach a moral lesson; we must live it. Children are deaf to our preaching but are watching intently the way in which *we* make moral choices. No amount of discussion, textbooks, or programs can hold a candle to a parent's witness of a real-life decision to do the right thing. When our children leave the realm of video games, movies, and television, and watch someone they know and love struggle with the decision to do good, they begin to connect the moral dots.

We are not born knowing what is wrong. We find it in two ways: first by observation and then by a natural law that pervades human life and society. We first observe and practice morality under the supervision of someone who is willing (for the sake of love) to lead us in the way of what is "good, right, and perfect." Then, the subtle lessons of the natural law reinforce and direct us. Natural law is not based on religious dogma and so on, but is generated from the experience of daily life. In the first years of life, we discover this law and see what is required of those who honor it. This natural law expresses a deep moral sense that rests within our reason. As we grow in our skill to reason, to develop cognitive skill, we discern in a completely natural way good and evil, love and hate, truth and the lie.

The relationship between a parent and a child, therefore, requires that parents lead lives of moral strength and explain to their children the reasons for their own actions. We have forgotten that these beautiful little souls are being formed by everything that happens around them, especially in the lives of their parents.

It was Jonathan, a young father, who realized this lesson in a most profound way. Driving twenty miles over the speed limit, he slowed down to the sixty-five-miles-per-hour limit when he saw a police car. His five-year-old daughter remarked from her car seat, "Daddy, you are allowed to cheat when there is no policeman to catch you." Jonathan told me later, "The lesson I was teaching my child was that it really isn't wrong if you do not get caught." That experience led him to see his actions through the eyes of a discerning five-year-old.

AFFIRM AND CORRECT

When children begin to imitate the witness of their parents, they need to be told that they are on the right track. Parents need to affirm a child's right behavior. Likewise, when children fail to do the right thing, a parent's explanation, with gentle but firm correction, is just as important. I believe that the underlying reason our children are drifting in a sea of moral apathy is that no one has taken the time to explain the impact the children's actions have on those around them.

Sports can be an ideal arena to teach—and learn—the effects of behavior. Team play requires that everyone do his or her part. Defense and offense work together for "good," which in sports is winning the game. When we can help children see that the same principle applies to life, we help them realize that everything a person does has an impact. The presence of moral coaches and teachers in our children's lives can be a real bonus.

If a coach is willing to take the lessons of the playing field into the arena of life, everyone is blessed.

I will never forget Jenny, a student of mine who was struggling and constantly in trouble in high school. I could not reach her no matter what I said or did. She always seemed to be breaking the rules, missing tests, losing her homework, not paying attention. Then she began playing varsity volleyball in her junior year. Teachers remarked that she had changed. It was as if Jenny was a totally different girl. The guidance counselor asked Jenny what had changed, and the teen replied, "Volleyball is teaching me that every player must carry her weight. Winners know how to care and do what is right. I am accountable for every choice I make, on the court and everywhere else." Through the young woman who coached her, Jenny learned a lesson that my religion class couldn't teach.

Parents are required to guide their children from infancy to adulthood in choosing what is right and correcting them when they fail. It takes a strong and steadfast commitment to do this work. It is so much easier to ignore behaviors—wrong and right—than it is to deal with them.

PROVIDE OPPORTUNITIES FOR CHILDREN TO SERVE OTHERS

While the world of sports is a great place to teach moral lessons, we can really up the teaching ante when we offer our children opportunities to serve others. Serving others shows children that life is not "all about me," that what they need and want does not come first at the cost of another. When any of us thinks that it is "all about me," we cannot comprehend the gospel challenge to "love others as we love ourselves," not to mention laying down our lives for another.

From an early age, children need to learn how to put aside what they need and want in order to give comfort and help to someone else. When the dimension of serving another is a part of a child's moral choices, the child experiences a new depth of understanding.

This dividing line was made quite obvious to me one day in a room full of preschoolers. Fifteen three-year-olds were gathered at the school where I minister. Eight trays each held a craft project. Some children rushed with no regard for anyone and took a tray; four children cried because they didn't get to go first; and three little ones watched and comforted those children who cried and waited. Those three children who provided solace were living in their own way the work of mercy to "comfort the afflicted." Someone had taught them how to serve.

SHARPEN THE LENS OF COMPASSION

Another easy way to teach making this "right" choice is to sharpen the child's lens of compassion. Parents and teachers can make an effort to point out in the daily lives of children when compassion is necessary. Too often, we adults as well as our children are so self-absorbed that we have no idea that another person is hurting, struggling, or needing help. There just doesn't seem to be much caring about another's plight in our dog-eat-dog society.

I experienced this most profoundly one day when I was driving my teenage son and his friends to a sports event. We witnessed a woman off the side of the road who had been pulled over by a police officer. She was sobbing and pleading with him. The boys, my son included, began to make fun of this "silly" woman who had lost control. I listened to their ridicule and then remarked to them, "Boys, you have no idea what is going on in that woman's life. What if she is worried about a family crisis, is struggling with unemployment, or something else terrible. This could have been the final straw for her." I then asked the boys to listen while I prayed for her. It was the first of many times when we prayed for someone in distress on the highway. I believe it was a foundational step in teaching my sons to never make a rash judgment and always try to respond with compassion.

The lens of compassion allows children to weigh their moral choices with the heart of God. When we can discern what to do based on the needs of someone else, we are able to see things as a loving Divine Parent sees them. It is slow work to turn the minds and hearts of children from focusing on their own needs to focusing on those of others. It begins with parents and teachers sharpening the lens and pointing out the moments of compassion.

EXPECT GOODNESS

Years ago when I was a singer in a renowned choir, the music director at the church told us that we will get what we expect out of our choir. "If we expect to sing like the best, we will be the best," he told us. That sounded fine to me until that director composed a solo written just for me that I knew was far beyond my vocal skill. I struggled with embarrassment and failure each week at practice. As the week of the performance approached, the director took me aside and simply said that he had written this part especially for my voice. He knew I could do it. I only needed to let go of my fear and sing. He expected me to be spectacular. That was all it took! I sang perfectly and everyone marveled at my skill.

That life lesson has stayed with me: we do get what we expect. If we hold the moral bar high for our children, they will rise to our expectations. If we make excuses for our children's immorality (and our own), we will keep our children from turning their backs on wrongdoing. When we expect children to do the right thing, care about others, and even put aside their own needs to serve others, they will come to believe that goodness is the norm. Breaking God's law then is just not an option. We do not lower our standards to fit the world's ways. This is a life lesson that takes on new meaning as our little ones grow into adolescents. Such behavior as being chaste won't make much sense if chastity has not been held up as the norm at home, regardless of the impurity that surrounds us in our culture.

KEEP OUR WORD

The final learned behavior that is a part of the groundwork of moral formation is teaching children to keep their word. In previous times the old saying "You are as good as your word" meant that once two people said something was going to happen and they shook hands on it, no written contract was required. Not so in our day, when lying and cheating are commonplace. When we have salespeople, politicians, even scientists and celebrities, making promises they do not keep, it is no wonder that our children do not understand the integrity of words. We must keep children (and adults) accountable for their words as well as their actions.

Bud, my neighbor, bought a car for his twenty-something daughter. She needed that car to get to her job, and she promised that each month she would make a "car payment." All went well for the first two months. Then, Bud received nothing, even after gentle and not-so-gentle reminders. It was obvious that Bud's daughter reneged on her promise to pay him back. I told Bud to let it go unless he was willing to alienate his daughter forever. Bud resigned himself to consider the car a gift. Yet, even now the relationship is estranged because both father and daughter are disappointed in a promise that failed to be kept.

When we seek and expect accountability, we will begin to see something strange start to happen: a renewed trust in our relationship as parent to child, student to teacher emerges. It is then a time for us to teach our children, from the bottom up, the skill of keeping and honoring words. We can begin by holding children to deadlines and curfews, by making certain that family chores are completed, by doing whatever it takes on a daily basis to believe that what we say is true. This basic skill seems so rudimentary, and yet, too many young ones have no idea that what people say to them and what they say to others must be truthful and full of consequence.

These few principles of teaching moral behavior will challenge any parent in the early years of a child's moral formation—and continue to challenge through young adulthood. It takes attention and constant surveillance by parents to stay on top of guiding the moral way. After all, the world seems to be against us parents at every turn.

As we try to write God's law on our hearts, we must remember that God is doing the writing, not us. So, we pray in the process and give in to grace. In the end we are simply God's instruments. We offer to our children what we have received from a loving and merciful God who protects and guides those he loves.

Remember

- Morality is a learned behavior. Moral lessons must first be taught at home. The great solution to teaching wrong from right is so simple that we miss it: we cannot preach a moral lesson; we must live it.

- When children begin to imitate the witness of their parents, parents need to affirm a child's right behavior. Likewise, when children fail to do the right thing, a parent's explanation, with gentle but firm correction, is just as important.

- Provide opportunities for your child to serve others.

- Teach your child to be compassionate.

- Expect good behavior of your child. Teach that being "good" is the best and preferred option.

- Keep integrity in all that you say. When you say it, mean it and keep true to your words.

Ponder

1. Recall a time when someone's moral example affected your life. How did you change your behavior as a result?

2. When did a time of serving others change your attitude toward those you served?

3. What are some moral laws by which you live?

4. What do you think contributes to the moral decline of our society? In what way can you work to improve our moral climate?

Exercise

Create a list of adjectives that describe your version of the moral child (e.g., honest, reliable) and a list of the immoral version (e.g., lying, cheating). Then make a list of children who are examples of the first list.

Pray

Wise and Gentle Parent,
guide those of us who care for children.
Give us clearer vision when confronted with
    confusion.
Strengthen our spiritual fiber when we must act on
    what we profess.
Change our weakness into courage as we insist on
    truth and justice.
And, Merciful God, remind us that love alone is the
    balm
that heals the wounds of damaged hearts. Amen.

CHAPTER 2

The Gift of Respect

Caroline's newborn daughter, Sophie, was twenty-three inches long, and so the pediatrician told Caroline that Sophie had the promise of being very tall. Caroline knew what that would mean: her daughter would be relegated to the end of lines in grade school, she would slump her shoulders and slouch while sitting so that she did not appear taller than the boys in her high school, and she would face a lifetime of feeling like a freak of nature because she was heads above everyone.

From the time of the doctor's prognosis, Caroline whispered in little Sophie's ear, "You are full of grace, hold your head high, and wow everyone with your beauty." Caroline made it her mission to respect Sophie's stature, to reinforce the special attribute of height as a gift meant only for the ballerina, the model, the person of immense talent. It was Caroline's respect for Sophie that caused the child to blossom into a shoulders-back, head-held-high, engaging woman of incredible confidence. Sophie, as an adult now, walks with poise as she leads the competition in international marketing—all thanks to the unwavering respect Caroline still gives her six-foot-two daughter.

One of the most important jobs of every parent is to culti-vate a child's self respect. When we treat children with an hon-est respect, we feed their souls. Moral children sense that goodness. Right thinking is the natural consequence of loving and respecting ourselves. When children understand from infancy that they are appreciated, lovable, and worthwhile, they will wish to love and respect others as they have been respected. We get a clue from Jesus' words, "Love others as you love your-self" (John 13:33–34).

We often miss the point of that statement, which is not as much about loving others as it is about loving ourselves. In fact, the first step in living a moral life and loving someone else as ourselves is to really love and care for ourselves first. Childhood formation is the testing ground of self-love, and it is parents who begin to teach the lesson of graced self-love. This testing ground occurs naturally in the family nest. In this place, where parents nurture and provide security, a child will either receive a blessing or a curse. Blessed children receive the knowledge that they are loved, appreciated, and called to use their gifts and talents for others. In contrast, children who are cursed get the message that a person must earn love. These children are rarely noticed and affirmed.

Carlos is a child who at age eight already had a criminal record. He had been violent in school and had been involved in petty theft incidents. Carlos had lived with a foster parent since he was abandoned at age two. What I noticed first about this beautiful little boy was that no one had ever bothered with him. He was just a number in a system of neglected faces. Carlos had presumed that no one loved him and that he was worthless. No adult in his life showed up at parent events, and he did not participate in extracurricular activities. So when his third-grade teacher impulsively reached out to Carlos, she did the simplest things: she asked Carlos to help her after school, she found him a grandparent tutor, she blessed him each day, and made a conscious effort to notice his presence and encourage him. Like a dying flower that was finally watered, Carlos began to flourish. The teacher chose to get involved. By May of his third-grade year, Carlos was placed in another third-grade family's home. The old Carlos seemed like a distant memory.

Every child needs to be validated, noticed, loved, and held high as God's delight. Without it, life is just a constant curse.

TREAT A CHILD WITH UNWAVERING RESPECT

We need to learn how to respect a child. It takes a conscious effort to see and affirm our children. After all, little ones cannot earn respect. We must choose to give it to them as a gift. There must be an understanding from the very beginning of our relationship with a child that we see their potential, their goodness, and, most of all, how "precious" in God's sight they are (Isa 43). It is a mindset that helps us listen to their thoughts and regard their presence with dignity. We choose to treat this child as valuable and as a contributing member of our circle of life. When we see children as persons with valuable ideas, talents that need to be nurtured, and even insights that escape us, then we begin to form relationships with children on the basis of mutual respect. It is primary to that relationship that we believe that this child brings something to us that we cannot receive from any other person, regardless of age or education.

I love seeing adults who honor children in this way. It seems that little ones flock to such people, especially if no one else gives them the time of day. Brian Cooney, a very popular and successful educator, retired from his position at Centre College as a philosophy professor. Because Brian knows how to respect young adults, his former students would often come back to the college to seek him out and tell him that he was one of their favorite professors. I didn't fully appreciate the respect and love Brian commanded until I observed him listening to a young man who had twice quit college and was returning at the age of twenty-eight to complete a degree. Brian listened and affirmed the man's story with genuine concern. It was as if the two men were engaged in a great adventure of success. Nowhere in Brian's demeanor was the slightest hint that failure was an option. He gave that young man a great gift that day: hope, encouragement, and respect. Looking back, many of us may remember just such a mentor teacher, a special person who stepped in, had faith in us, and called us to greater things.

THE FOUR PRINCIPLES OF RESPECT

Learning to respect others isn't easy in a world in which we are taught to think of our needs and pleasures as a first priority. It helps to remove ourselves from the day-to-day challenges of parenting and to purposefully analyze how we can support each child in the effort to build the child's self-respect.

We need to ask and answer honestly the question concerning teaching respect: Do I understand my child's hopes and dreams? How can I clearly offer support for the long-term and immediate goals that we (parent + child) have created? How can I offer constructive criticism and praise to my child? What can I do to reassure my child that I will always stand by him or her when being moral proves difficult?

Here are four very simple principles that underscore the process of teaching respect:

1. **Share a child's dreams.** When parents and child have never dreamed together, there is an unspoken belief that those dreams are not worth much. Parents who listen with an open heart and a sense of wonder when their child honors them with their dreams enter into the world of possibilities. It is here that we can say, "What you envision is good." "Your potential has no limits." When a child believes that "all things are possible with God," he sees himself as honorable, and in some mysterious way, as a part of a greater whole. It is no longer "just me" thinking up impossible schemes but "me and those who love me" (including God) fashioning wonderful possibilities.

   We can join our children in their visions and dreams of their future by giving in to some stargazing. Quite literally, we need to find sacred moments when we look at the night sky, watch a fire, and so on, and allow our child to tell us her dreams for tomorrow and for the years ahead. Listening to children's dreams with acceptance and affirmation helps children see that we believe in their potential. It is our job to help them see this potential.

No matter your child's age (from infancy to adult), it is important to put aside time every month for dream time with your child. I do this by meeting one evening a month for one-on-one conversation and supper with each of the four souls God has given me to form. I listen to my children (all adults with children of their own now), and they talk, and in every way possible I encourage and affirm their stories. We have been through a few crises and lifted numerous toasts to their victories. These for me have been times of pure magic!

2. **Set goals with a child and help him or her to achieve them.** We all need to feel like we are headed in the right direction. Children especially need to be encouraged by their progress and corrected when they wander off the path. Nothing is more discouraging than working hard and not recognizing progress. Simple, short-term goals underscore progress and a "job well done."

A kitchen chart that identifies chores completed, a school project that is planned and executed, an audition for a play, or a tryout for a sports team, and so on, all help children to experience satisfaction in a job well done. As the adult partner in goal setting, it is important that we name the challenge that is ahead. We must be very specific in how we identify a job well done: "Getting a passing grade on the next math test," "emptying the dishwasher each afternoon," and so on. By articulating clearly a task and our expectations for that task, we teach children that everything they do has value and that when they succeed they are capable and valued.

But what happens when a child fails in the effort? Just like teaching a toddler to walk, every time a child misses the mark, falls in frustration, and so on, our job is to be there and pick up our child. In fact, educators tell us that students learn more when they fail a test than when they breeze through the content. Failure can help us all to regroup and rethink with a stronger effort than ever. It is at these moments of disillusionment that we parents pour out a blessing on our children. We must tell our children in no uncertain terms that we believe in them and that we mean to stand with them as they try again.

As children grow into accepting and setting more challenging goals, the experience of their early years of completing simple objectives will pay off. They have made investments in the "respect bank" over those childhood years. Now, as these young adults attend college and venture out into the world of careers and marriage, they can be rooted in the belief that they are worthwhile and that those they interact with deserve the same respect.

Another valuable aspect of goal setting is creating a clear boundary for what is expected. The finish line is necessary. Moses wandered around that desert because he didn't have a map. Looking for the promised land of our own life goals is much easier when we name the destination and keep our eye on it. Boundaries foster a security that says "I know who I am and where I am going."

3. **Be generous with honest praise.** As we guide children into feeling good about themselves and knowing their potential, we must work at telling them when they have succeeded. Parents, teachers, and coaches must change the lens of observation and direction: when a child does well, shows promise, and so on, we need to acknowledge this aloud. Too many times we just assume that children know that they did well. We must give a child an honest word of praise as often as possible. There is that natural tendency to quickly tell them that their grades need to improve, or that if they had practiced more often the piano lesson would have been more rewarding. Our culture loves to criticize and tear down. Our job with a child is to do just the opposite: praise and build up.

When we let a child see that we notice him and appreciate his goodness, we are really blessing him. Remember Jesus' baptism in the Jordan when a voice from heaven said, "This is my beloved Son in whom I am well pleased." That was a simple blessing from his Father. God wants us to do the same for our children. The more we bless others, the more the others see themselves as blessed, good, and worthy. In contrast, when we belittle or deride the other, we are literally cursing them. It has been my experience that children who are cursed in this way continue the practice with their own children. If we were never praised as a child, or worse, were cursed by someone we loved, we should break the cycle and choose to bless.

One Sunday when my family gathered for supper, I noticed that my daughter-in-law had lost weight after the recent birth of her child. I knew she had worked hard to shed those baby pounds. I silently thought how good she looked. With a nudge from the Holy Spirit, I said what I was thinking, "You have lost weight. You look beautiful!" My daughter-in-law beamed with pride over her accomplishment as all the family congratulated her. All it took was for me to say out loud what I was thinking. I blessed that beautiful young mom, and she received the blessing like a priceless treasure.

4. **Stand behind a child when he or she is persecuted for righteousness.** This is where the rubber meets the road for parents. It is fine to talk to children about doing the right thing but far more powerful to support them when they are chided and put down for their right choices. In my view, the greatest reason our children decide to not act justly is that they fear being criticized by their peers. Social pressure to conform to the accepted norm, regardless of how wrong or right it is, seems to be the major factor in determining the moral choices children make. A child's desire to "fit in" is the greatest priority. I can remember my father saying "If every-

one else jumped off a bridge, would you jump too?" My answer was always "yes" until I matured enough to respect my own judgments.

When a child is not respected by those by whom they wish to be accepted, the child needs us to help restore that respect by standing with her and letting her know that she did the right thing, and no price is too great to pay. These are the times when self-respect may be all a child has to hold on to, and we need to tell the child so. Too many children are victimized by bullies and aggressive peers who want nothing more than to demoralize the "do-gooder." As parents and adult authorities, we must protect children from being victimized and bullied.

Without respect for others and for self, no child will thrive and learn to behave in a moral way. As parents we must model respect for others always. And more importantly, we must respect ourselves by living a healthy life in body, mind, and spirit.

Remember

- Cultivate your child's self respect. When children understand from infancy that they are appreciated, lovable, and worthwhile, they will wish to love and respect others as they have been respected.

- Respect and affirm your child. See his or her potential and goodness and acknowledge how precious in God's sight your child is.

- Share your child's dreams.

- Set goals with your child and help him or her to achieve them.

- Be generous with honest praise of your child.

- Stand behind your child when he or she is persecuted for righteousness.

Ponder

1. How would you describe self-respect to an adolescent?

2. What do you think can contribute to a child's poor self-image?

3. Who were some adults who helped you fulfill your dreams? How did they help you?

4. Share a time when a child had to stand up for what was right in the face of ridicule.

5. What can coaches and teachers do to affirm and encourage children in an honest way?

Exercise

Begin to keep a journal of moments of honest praise: when your child does something worthy of your praise and encouragement, write it down and note the child's response. Someday give this journal to your child as a gift.

Pray

Come, Holy Spirit,
blow your breath through me

that I may speak your words of encouragement
and listen with your caring heart.
Shower upon my child the grace of unwavering
    respect,
for herself/himself, for others, and for you. Amen.

CHAPTER 3

Feelings vs. Reason

The days are long past when "Because I said so" is a sufficient response to a child's "Why?" about a behavior. In fact, recent opinion holds that people born after 1982 will not blindly obey; they need to understand the reason for complying.

In a time when moral fortitude is tested every day, it is second nature to do what is easy rather than what is right. The very reason for doing something could very well be that it was easier than doing the "right" thing. The challenge that remains for everyone who forms a child's conscience is to teach from birth to adulthood that reason rather than feelings must temper our moral choices. That means that each of us must take a giant step backward and examine just why we do what we do.

WHY DO WE DO WHAT WE DO?

Explaining the reason for a choice seems so elementary. Yet, in many cases, we simply do something because we have always done it. The story of a young granddaughter who wanted to make pot roast just like grandma's applies: Julie, in the first months of her marriage, was determined to carry on the family's culinary traditions. She asked her mother for grandma's recipe for pot roast. The recipe began with "Buy a five-pound rump roast and cut one inch off both ends and discard." Julie asked her mother why the ends were cut off. Could it be a secret to the delicious pot roast or the perfect gravy? Did it cause the juices to reenter the meat from the bottom of the pan? Julie's mom said that she had no idea and suggested a visit to grandma for the answer. Julie approached grandma with the question and received an astounding response: "My mother's roasting pan was too small. I had to cut the ends off to get the roast in the pan." For decades, two generations of cooks had cut off the ends of the roast for the sake of a small roasting pan that was long gone. With laughter and new insight, Julie began a new tradition of great pot roast with the ends in place.

Little choices need to be understood and explained as much as big, important choices. We can begin by looking at the instructions we give to children. We must offer with any instructions the consequences of a wrong choice: "When you leave your toys on the floor, someone could step on them and break them," or "When you touch the stove, you could burn your fingers and that would hurt a lot." During the toddler stage, it helps to make the consequences very personal to a child: "When you choose this…, you will experience this…" As a child matures, the consequences can be less personal; for example,

"When you leave your toys on the floor, Daddy could step on them and hurt his foot."

This explanation also establishes clear boundaries for developing consciousness. When what we choose causes harm, we come to understand that this is a poor choice—that choosing what is good rather than what is hurtful is the better path. As the experience of understanding why something is good is lived out and the boundaries become clear, a child begins to connect the moral dots in a most basic way. Rather than doing the right thing and not knowing why, we start to see that easy is not necessarily the best reason to do what we do. Even though it feels good at the moment, there are long-term consequences for each choice.

RULES PROVIDE STRUCTURE

Liam was six years old and the terror of his first-grade class. He couldn't sit still. He didn't seem to care about sharing. He lost his papers and couldn't remember his homework assignments. The school psychologist was called and proclaimed that Liam was a "rules guy." In his wisdom, Dr. Fred, as the students called him, told Liam's parents that Liam needed structure. Liam did not have an attention deficit disorder, and there was no other explanation for being a young rebel. Liam was made for military school, said Dr. Fred, as he advised the parents that ten pushups after disregarding a rule would do Liam wonders. But military school for Liam was not an option, so what next? Dr. Fred advised Liam's parents to put in place a strict regimen of rules. The parents, teacher, and all those who loved Liam enforced consistently the daily routine that included a penalty for ignoring a rule. The penalty was immediate: time out to rethink the choice plus a loss of a privilege, such as study hall instead of recess or no computer time that evening. Those rules reinforced Liam's world, and he prospered. He felt comfortable for the first time in his life. When Liam realized that he was a "rules guy," he became attracted to athletics where rules abounded and counted. Playing by the rules made sense to Liam and helped him see why rules also made sense in the other areas of his life.

Not every child is a "rules guy," yet the strategy of offering structure in a child's life points the way to a child's positive formation. While many would say that a child needs to do what pleases him and that structure restricts creativity, we should view rules as a gift rather than a hindrance to formation. The debate will continue, and we must also realize that not every child needs a lot of structure. But when we embrace a sense of order and structure, we are then free to leave the concerns of daily care and discover a world of creativity, imagination, and learning.

It was this same principle that led monastics like St. Benedict to create the "Rule," a written set of behaviors that structured a monk's daily personal and communal life in a monastery. When the ways of keeping wellness, fairness, and generosity are observed, our spirits are free to embrace the higher things. This could be, perhaps, a prime reason why so many people flock to a monastery to sort out life's issues and soak up some much-needed inner peace.

RULES EMPOWER CHILDREN

We can look at rules in two ways: as chains that bind or as tools for success. Often when I speak about this topic, I will ask the folks gathered: "How many of you as children sat into the night in front of a plate of cold lima beans because you refused to eat them?" Inevitably the room bursts into laughter, and the hands fly up. Those poor lima beans have taken a bum rap! As we sat in our childhood kitchens, staring at the green meanies, our mothers chanted, "You will never know whether you like them if you never taste them." One woman in an audience admitted to me after my talk, "I refused to eat lima beans for thirty years. Then I tasted one and found out that they are delicious!"

When we offer a rule to a child, it is far better to teach that the reason for the rule is powerful and contains a grace rather than explain the rule in negative language. With the lima bean saga, it might have been better to explain the dietary rule, "You must eat your lima beans because they are little gems full of good stuff that will make you stronger and full of energy." Lima bean trials are more often battles of wills between parent and child than a testing ground for healthy nutrition. In all of our rule teaching, we should let compromise and charity prevail.

A dynamic teacher, Anna, taught sixth graders the Ten Commandments in an innovative manner that still resonates in the souls of her students long after they left sixth grade. Anna turned "Thou shall not kill" into the more positive "Thou shall protect and prosper life." Anna saw the light go on in the eyes of her students as she empowered them to live with a challenge. She uncovered a dignity in her class discussions of the commandments. Anna said that what became so clear was that we have a choice to rise above the minimum and do something greater. A rule in its essence is never meant to confine behavior; rather, rules call us to discover the deeper good within.

CONNECT A CHILD WITH CHILDREN WHO ARE OLDER AND YOUNGER

A great way for children to learn the value of rules and the process of understanding them is to rub elbows with their peers. There is nothing quite like seeing rules in action to understand the reason for doing what is right. Many of us remember learning the facts of life from an older friend. Parents, as "experts," can do all the right things and tell a child the beautiful story of human life and how it begins, but the person we wanted to hear this from was most often an older kid. It seemed that the true slant on turning into an adult male or female had to come from the mouths of one of our own. We simply trusted our peers' opinions more than any grownup's. A dear childhood friend, Mary Lynn, told me the whole story of human procreation one day during fifth-grade recess. It seemed ridiculous to me that my parents would do such things with each other, but Mary Lynn was an authority that I respected and believed, so what she described must have been true.

This attitude plays out in peer ministry for youth. The best spiritual mentors for teens are older teens and young adults. When we surround our young people with role models they can relate to and who witness gospel values, we experience the best of both worlds. Our task as parents and shapers of a child's moral behavior is to help our children surround themselves with models of moral behavior rather than with any witnesses of immoral behavior. It takes constant diligence to protect young adults from harm. Knowing who they keep company with is essential.

Allowing a younger sibling to be part of an older sibling's circle is also important for the older child. When we challenge our child to set an example for someone younger, we allow important questions to enter the older child's mind: "What will the little one think about me when I choose to do the wrong thing? How can I explain the best way for us to play? How can I protect the little one from harm?"

Suddenly roles are reversed, and the older child becomes a mentor. There is a natural desire to pass on what we know to those who come behind us. In passing along to a younger person the reason for doing what is right, the mentor child owns the rule in a whole new way. No longer is it something "I have to do because someone else says so." Now it becomes "I am choosing to do it for myself because I believe it is right, and I want a younger person to understand and accept what I believe."

This dynamic of relating to peers is the testing ground for integrating reason into decision making. A child belongs to a social structure that is outside the domain of her relationship with parents, teachers, and other adults. Among one's own companions, where the words of the rules are played out in the child's reality, what once seemed foreign is translated into reasoning that is familiar to her.

OPEN-ENDED QUESTIONS

We can guide our children into reflecting on their choices with open-ended questions. That means that we learn the fine art of communicating with our child about their moral choices. Open-ended questions help to develop moral reasoning because there are no definitive answers to questions like: "How did you feel when you gave up your place in line to your handicapped friend?" "What is your best reason for keeping up with study goals?" These kinds of questions offer a child another way to evaluate the choices they have made. Too often we just react for good or bad without realizing the results of what we did.

Parents and other mentors have a gift that their children do not have: we can use our intuitive skills to comprehend the deeper reasons for doing the right thing. Children do not have, and even some adults never develop, this skill. I have met many men and women who have never asked themselves these important questions. They lead lives on the surface. They simply never answer questions that deal with feelings or the impact of an event on the spirit. Poetry eludes them, the moral of a story is not a concern, and so on. Thus, teaching our children to be introspective has great value. We are teaching them to see with the eyes of the soul.

ENCOURAGE A CHILD TO THINK INDEPENDENTLY

While children of this age want to know why a rule exists, every age deals with peer-group pressure. If everyone else is jumping off the dangerous proverbial bridge, every kid with at least two good friends is jumping too. Our job is to convince our children to think on their own. This is a tough order that will require believing that our personal opinion is more valuable than the collective nod. One of the most important blessings we can give a child is to tell them that their opinion has value. Even if everyone they know disagrees, what they think matters.

Carmelo was the only young man in the neighborhood who stayed in high school after he turned sixteen. The guys he had grown up with had formed a new gang. They dressed alike and roamed the streets every night while Carmelo stayed inside and did homework. When I asked Carmelo what kept him from following the other boys' path, he said simply, "Grandma taught me to follow my heart, and my heart says gang life is death." Since that conversation three years have passed, and Carmelo has left the hood and is a student in a community college. Two of his friends were killed in neighborhood drug wars. God chooses strange prophets.

The gentle balance between feelings and reason is an acquired skill. Throughout our life journey the balance of these two come into play repeatedly. It is the job of those of us who mentor children to show them to honor both their hearts and their minds and come to keep a rule that reflects both the letter and spirit of the law. It is not an easy task. It calls us all to look deeper than the surface of why we do what we do, to understand both the reason and compassion behind a choice.

Remember

- Explain to your child the reasons for little and big choices. Offer with any instructions the consequences of a wrong choice and a right choice.

- Use rules to add structure to your child's life.

- Teach your child that the reason for a rule is powerful and that it contains a grace. Avoid explaining a rule in negative language.

- Surround your child with role models of different ages that he or she can relate to and who witness gospel values. Teens can be especially effective role models with younger children.

- Ask your child open-ended questions that help him or her to reflect on right and wrong choices.

- Encourage your child to think independently and to know that his or her opinion has value.

Ponder

1. Growing up, what was a family rule in your house? Was it difficult to abide by this rule?

2. What are some rules that make your life easier?

3. Share a time when an older child served as a mentor to a younger child.

4. What are some open-ended questions that help you to understand the value of a rule?

5. What are some rules in church and society that are not understood?

Exercise

Gather your family and create ten commandments for your house. Ask yourselves: what ten rules will make our lives more loving, safer, peaceful? Post the Big Ten and try to honor them.

Pray

Release in me, O Wisdom,
the gift of sharing

with those in my care
what I know about what is good, right, and perfect.
May I pass on your torch
of loving a good rule,
seeking its meaning,
and being faithful to the truth. Amen.

Emotions Are Important

While it is important to teach our children to think through the right and wrong of things, it is equally important to teach them how to use feelings to season moral decisions. Having a hunch about something cannot be ignored. But just what does it mean to have instinct, a gut feeling, or an unexplained desire to go or behave in a certain way?

Humans are distinguished by our ability to have feelings. These feelings seem to be a component of a deeper self. The soul is within each of us. That true authentic self that resides within our depth is the place where genuine feelings originate. There we find the mystical side of each of us. Perhaps there, in that unblemished heart within, is where the Divine One resides, guiding us with a wordless sense of doing what is good.

Whatever we call "soul," it has a role to play in the way we perceive what is the best and right choice. We are asked to pass on
that soul connection to our children.

TUNING INTO AND NAMING A CHILD'S FEELINGS

Many people live their whole lives and never know how
they feel about things. They live on the surface and cannot
process common reactions of happiness, satisfaction, fear, anger,
and so on. In fact, such folks do not even comprehend—or
speak!—the emotional language that is second nature to poets,
mystics, and imaginative minds. Early on we must help our children to see with the eyes of the soul. This soul language enables
all of us to perceive the presence of something or Someone
beyond the physical world. It is in Antoine de Saint Exupéry's
The Little Prince that it is expressed so well: "What is essential
is invisible to the eye." When our children begin to see beyond
the surface, they can understand that the deeper meaning of
events and decisions impact life. It is a deeper view beyond the
obvious into the consequences of choice. When a child does not
have this understanding, he or she develops what the Old
Testament calls "stony hearts." Feelings are foreign, and conversations of the heart are very difficult.

Jenna, a bright three-year-old, started attending church
with her parents on Sundays. The family sat up front, and Jenna
soon became enthralled with all the sacred images and beautiful
decorations. When the service began, however, and everyone
stood and recited the "Our Father," Jenna looked at her
mommy and asked, "Why are these people saying the same

thing, and just who are they talking to?" At that moment Jenna's parents began to explain "things unseen" to their child. We begin to teach our children at an early age to believe in things unseen, to start showing them how to connect with intuitive concepts like love, fear, sorrow, and compassion. It is in the world of imagination where we introduce our sacred language. As we explain the unseen God to whom we pray, our children learn that the dialogue with God is a part of a nonmaterial world. Also, that sacred world is kept in the rhythm of intuitive experiences. It is here that we make that great leap into believing things we cannot measure or see. Giving our children an understanding of these sacred things is one of the greatest gifts we can give them, but it is also one of the most difficult.

We should always encourage children to enter their own make-believe world. All too soon they will leave this imaginary arena of visions and myths that come from each little one's spirit. It is pure balm for the soul when they will later try to grasp the essence of things unseen. My children still delight in the imaginary saga we shared each bedtime about a pony that took them on journeys to wonderful foreign worlds. "Pony Hunt" knocked on the bedroom window, and the child and pony rode together through the sky to the jungle or the desert for adventure and mystery. As parent and child together, we were learning the mystical skill of finding the sacred in the ordinary. In hindsight, I think my children taught me more than I taught them.

The easiest way to enter this unseen, intuitive world is to begin to identify the feelings that a child experiences. Simple reinforcements during everyday moments help children understand their feelings: "When you have to leave the playground at recess and return to the classroom, you feel sad..."; "This is a

happy day for you...”; or “Sometimes the dark can scare us....”
The adult skill of naming how we feel comes to us gradually but
must be taught. When I meet adults who boast that they have
never cried or cannot understand why their spouse wants to talk
about how the love they share is important, and so on, I see that
these people simply never learned the language of feelings and
their importance.

Parents are tasked with forming not only their child’s body
and mind but also the child’s spirit. When we neglect teaching a
child what feelings mean, how a feeling can bring joy or pain,
and how to name feelings in words, we have neglected the
child’s spirit. Children who have never learned how to identify
how they feel will never be able to comprehend how their feelings affect what they do.

BEING AWARE OF OTHER'S FEELINGS

The early years of a child’s formation are the time to name
emotions, but later years are when it is time to identify those
same feelings in others. Initially, little ones believe that the entire
world rotates around their needs and desires. Around age four,
children begin to notice others and learn social skills. This is the
time when we need to teach our children to understand how
their behavior impacts other people. What we are doing is
stretching young hearts and minds to connect the consequences
of their actions. The intricate balance of peace and wellbeing
requires that the needs of others are honored. Learning to see a
situation through the eyes of someone else can impact moral
development.

One day I was watching Colin, a four-year-old boy, squashing ants on his driveway with his foot. I asked, "Colin, why are you killing those ants?" He said, "Because it is fun." I responded, "It might be fun for you. But I'll bet the ant doesn't like it." Colin kept killing ants, totally disregarding my inquiry. Then I took a risk and asked, "Colin, how would you feel if a big giant ant came out from behind the garage and stepped on you?" Instantly, Colin stopped his ant squashing and said to me, "I would be afraid, and I wouldn't like it." While I worried that my question might scare my little charge, it was clear that he understood that we were talking about an imaginary ant and that he had nothing to fear. We then started laughing, and I proclaimed that day as "Be Kind to Ants Day." We gave the driveway ants a small piece of Colin's peanut butter and jelly sandwich, and Colin was fascinated with the parade of hungry ants. What we had experienced was a modern parable for a four-year-old.

While I would like to tell you that once you explain to a four-year-old that caring about others' feelings is important the child will never venture into self-centered behavior again, the fact is that all of us stray from "loving others as we love ourselves." The best we can do is to be vigilant. Rather than engaging in an academic discussion about being thoughtful and caring for other's feelings, the best approach with a child is often to allow situations to come to the forefront and then look at how those involved were feeling. The evening TV news, movies, books, sporting events, and even school events can offer a perfect resource for teaching about others' feelings.

This is the proving ground for raising a moral child. If this lesson about recognizing others' feelings is never learned, we will have formed adults who cannot comprehend that hurting others is wrong. They will believe that as long as their actions are pleasing, convenient, and cause no harm to themselves, what they do is acceptable and even morally good.

LET A CHILD KNOW HOW YOU FEEL

So often we really do not have to work hard at teaching this: everyday life becomes the playground of moral exercise. Teachers, mentors, and parents can do their best work by practicing a little humility.

I grew up believing that my parents never did anything wrong and never were weak in any way. It wasn't until my mother was in the last chapter of her life that I discovered all the pain and hurt that she had suppressed so that her children would have a happy childhood. She shared with me in those final days her story of a life filled with all the emotions of motherhood and marriage. While her selflessness was admirable, it made her a tough act to follow. I believed that really good women never felt afraid, sad, or ashamed, much less joyful, courageous, or proud. I know now that the best way to explain to a child how feelings connect to making life's decisions is to model the experience for our children. After all, most children want to grow up to be just like their parents.

We should look at most daily events as excellent teaching moments, such times as when the pork roast burns and Mom laughs as she resorts to cooking hot dogs for supper, when Dad yells at the entire family after the cat shreds the sofa upholstery because no one was minding the family pet, when Dad wins the golf tournament and wants to celebrate his victory with his golf buddies instead of going to his daughter's school play, when we arrive late to pick up our son from soccer practice because we had to "do just one more thing," when the new baby sleeps through the night and everyone else does too. Each moment is a time to declare our feelings.

GET PHYSICAL

One of the most precious things we can give our children is a physical demonstration of how we feel about them. Children who are kissed and hugged seem to flourish. There is something very powerful about touch. When children are lovingly embraced, they know something that no amount of words can express. We have all heard the importance of holding infants and know that babies who are deprived of human touch fail to thrive.

This lesson really hit home when I was working in Guatemala one summer and joined a group of priests, sisters, and laywomen to visit a hospital. When our group arrived at the hospital, the sister in charge warned us that we would experience a painful sight, and then she asked us to spend the next few hours holding abandoned children who were physically handicapped. When she opened the doors to a large room, I saw over two hundred cribs holding these little ones. For the next few hours we simply held the children, as Sister told us that there was no medicine as powerful as our touch. While emotionally spent at the end of our time there, I realized that within each of us is a very powerful gift—the gift of becoming to a child the hands and heart of a loving God. It is the very first way that a child knows God.

When we parent our own children, it is so important to show them our love. As they grow older, we can be sure that our outward display of affection will embarrass them. But I encourage you to take the risk and never stop saying, "I love you," or hugging and kissing your children. We are teaching children that the way we feel for one another is to be reverenced and proclaimed. Many of us come from family backgrounds where a show of affections was discouraged. Fathers and sons shook hands and never embraced, hugs were stiff, and kissing was forbidden. It will take a little courage to start breaking the no-touch rule. But the alternative is raising children who come to believe that feelings should be kept out of relationships.

This was so evident in one family that I know whose father seldom showed any feelings toward his sons except to discipline them. He was particularly hard on his eldest child, Mike, and was always quick to tell Mike what he could have done better and what he didn't do right. But on the day Mike left home to begin active military service with the very real possibility of going to war overseas, the father embraced his son and cried and told Mike to be careful. He then drove Mike to the recruiting office. It was a powerful message to Mike—and the rest of the family—that Mike was indeed loved by his dad, even if saying so was late in coming in Mike's life.

We can begin showing our feelings for others by using family comings and goings as the time to greet each other with a word and embrace. The door becomes a reminder that we need to affirm our love for each other as we leave each other and come home again. Husbands and wives need to model the gesture by never failing to kiss each other at the door and say, "I love you." Whether the children observe this greeting or not, the very practice begins to establish a habit that will quickly become second nature. No one ever comes or leaves my house without the warmth of a hug and a loving greeting. My children just assume that loving families always greet each other with love.

Another holy moment for a kiss is at bedtime. A kiss on a child's forehead and a little prayer for a peaceful night's sleep reminds children of a secure and holy love that surrounds them.

STORY TIME

Books and movies that talk about feelings are another wonderful way to bring feelings into focus. It is always easier to watch another person deal with emotions such as anger and fear than to deal with our own moments of darkness. In like manner, seeing another person experience joy, laughter, and playfulness validates our own experiences. Children need to understand that their good and bad moments are not unique, that all of us share the same feelings and reactions to life's moments. Realizing that others share the same or similar burdens and happy times, a child becomes less hesitant to talk with others about the feelings he or she is experiencing.

The best way to find books about feelings is to consult your child's language arts teacher, school psychologist, or a children's librarian who possess lists of books sorted for each grade level and often by subject category. Many books are available that help children deal with tough topics like grief, fear of the darkness, fear of abandonment, abuse, bullying, and so on. Before offering a book to a child, read it first so that you know who the characters are and what the situations have to say and how the book might speak to your child's circumstances. When we lead a child to understand feelings, we must have a clear idea of where we are going. An added benefit to reading children's literature is that we often gain as much insight into our own emotions as we will ever impart to our child. The power of books to help children understand and deal with their emotions was never so evident to me as when I met Carly, a third-grader devastated when her beloved Grammy died. No amount of consoling seemed to heal Carly's broken, grieving heart—until her godmother found a book on saying goodbye to someone you love. Each week Carly and her godmother would read the book together and talk about missing Grammy. The little ten-year-old girl in the book wrote letters to her grandmother and mailed them to heaven. By the time the pages of the book were well worn, Carly had written to Grammy many times about her hurt and sadness. Carly, now fifteen, credits that experience for helping her heal, and she still keeps that well-worn book in her night stand drawer.

Movies too are a good source for validating feelings. A family movie night followed by pizza and talk time can be a lot of fun and a wonderful way to deal with tough issues. The best place to find these movies is from other parents and teachers as well as by reading reviews online and in print by reviewers who evaluate the movies according to Christian values and morals. As with books for children, always view the movie before your children see it. While many movies have great lessons for dealing with feelings, they can also contain material that you may find objectionable for your child. You do not want to be caught by surprise.

Feelings are powerful and good—if we and our children identify them honestly and learn to use our feelings in addition to our reasoning to make right choices.

Remember

- Begin to teach your child at an early age to believe in things unseen, to start showing him or her how to connect with intuitive concepts like love, fear, sorrow, and compassion.

- Allow situations to come to the forefront and then look at how those involved were feeling. The evening TV news, movies, books, sporting events, and even school events can offer a perfect resource for teaching about your child's and others' feelings.

- Look at most daily events as excellent teaching moments. Each moment is a time to declare our feelings.

- Show physical demonstration of how you feel about your child—with kisses, hugs, pats on the back, and so on.

- Use books and movies that talk about feelings as a wonderful resource to bring feelings into focus. Consult with teachers, school psychologists, and children's librarians as well as online reviews for what to choose.

Ponder

1. How would you describe happiness and sadness to a small child?

2. Share an incident when a child became aware of how their actions affected another. When did another person's actions hurt or encourage you?

3. With whom do you find it most easy to share your feelings? Why?

4. Is your family comfortable with physical expressions of love? How can you encourage ways of sharing feelings in your family?

5. What children's book or movie do you remember that taught you or your child a lesson about feelings?

Exercise

Find online or print images that express emotions for you. Paste the images in a journal and reflect on why these images speak to you. *(This exercise is also a great project with children.)*

Pray

Lord God, you have created me with both mind and
    heart.
Temper my wisdom with the ways of the heart.
May the law you have written on my heart
be seasoned with love, joy, and delight.
Take all my fear, regret, and sadness into your
    merciful hands
so that I may experience
the healing balm of your wisdom. Amen.

CHAPTER 5

Consequences Are Real

On the day a child is born, the parents look at their precious baby and silently vow to protect this beautiful soul from all harm. Almost immediately we begin to realize that we cannot keep that promise. Real life has consequences, and sometimes those consequences are painful. Dirty diapers happen. Colic happens. An infant's life from its very first days undermines the parents' desire to create a perfect, pain-free life for their child. We still hold on to the idea, however, that we want to do everything possible to give our children a life devoid of hard times, pain, and disappointment. We just cannot help ourselves—it is the nature of love to protect and care for the beloved. So, we start to run interference for our child. We convince ourselves that we can avoid the consequences of a bad choice or a mistake by fixing it before our child is hurt or must bear up under a penalty. In reality, we do the child a grave injustice because the child never learns that every action has a necessary and unavoidable consequence.

I remember serving on the advisory board of a school system in a very wealthy town. The high school was having a serious drug problem and asked the board to offer suggestions on ways to deal with the problem. I suggested sending dogs that sniff out drugs in lockers at a time when the school was closed. Then the school would know which students were involved. I was not prepared for the reaction I received from the police chief and the school staff: "Oh, we cannot do that because it would implicate some of our better families!" I was shocked at this double standard. The rich kids were to be protected from consequences of possession of drugs. What the school wanted the board to recommend was a way to stop the drugs in the school without holding the students responsible. The psychologists, ministers, and youth counselors at that meeting knew that there was no hope for a resolution unless boundaries and consequences were upheld regardless of social status.

DISCIPLINE IS NOT ARBITRARY BUT IT CAN BE FLEXIBLE

The place to start as we establish an understanding of consequences is a firm yet loving method of discipline. The rules are the rules. Everyone needs to be on board about what constitutes acceptable behavior and what violates the rule. Not only do we need to know what the rule is, we need to know the consequences for breaking the rule. While the letter of the law is not the only consideration in discipline (there is always room for a flexible response to a broken rule), it is very important for adults and children alike to know what happens when a child crosses the line.

Nearly every child encounters rules, whether the rules are family rules, school rules, sports rules, workplace rules, and so on. Rules are a part of a child's life. Such codes of behavior originate within the community in which they will be practiced. Family rules should come from each house and be decided upon in the family unit. What is a sacred practice in one family may not even be considered in another.

At Jenna's house everyone is expected promptly at the dinner table at 6:00 p.m. No one is permitted to sit at the dinner table wearing a ball cap or dirty clothes. Hands must be washed, and feet must be in shoes. In comparison, at Noah's house, supper is served buffet style from the kitchen island. Each family member grabs a plate and eats informally in the family room. Table meals are reserved for Sundays and holidays. The only supper rule is that if you're not going to be home for the meal, you need to let mom know.

This comparison illustrates that there is no absolute wrong or right way to eat together. The family tradition and style dictate what works in each house.

Just as parents strive to determine family rules with the consensus of all the family members, so too should parents strive to determine with the family the consequences for breaking a family rule. Family meetings offer a perfect venue for discussing and establishing a system of rules and consequences. Parents should meet first and be in agreement concerning which rules are important and the consequences of a broken rule. Every year (at least) the family should come together to revisit the discussion about family rules because family life changes quickly as children get older and their involvement in school and extracurricular activities intensifies. Other circumstances that can radically affect a family's daily life include, for example, a grandparent moving in, a teenager getting a driver's license, mom returning to work, dad losing a job, and so on. When the family meets, the consequences should be negotiated and spelled out for everyone to understand.

Naomi understood that her parents asked that she limit her cell phone use until homework was completed on school nights. When Mom caught Naomi texting at her desk instead of studying for a geometry test, the consequences were immediate. Mom put out her hand, and Naomi placed the phone in it. The phone would be returned in three days. When I asked Naomi how she felt about losing her cell phone, she told me that she had broken a family rule, and she knew what would happen. She was mad at herself for giving in to the temptation but respected Mom for holding up the rule. Naomi said that it was the discussion at the family meeting when she had agreed to the consequences that kept her from "going ballistic" with her mom.

Parents need to administer consequences with their heart as well as with their head. This is where flexibility comes in. When a child breaks curfew because the parent driver was late, it is obvious that there is no infraction of the curfew rule. When a child deliberately stays out past curfew and does not call to be excused, the rule applies. We parents need to form a united front in these matters. All of us have been victims of "Dad said it was alright" when Mom was never included in the conversation. Communication is so necessary in daily life in a family. Parents cannot and should not presume that everyone in the family is on the same page regarding rules and consequences. Punishment must meet three criteria:

1. **The punishment should be appropriate to the crime.** If the crime is not completing a school assignment on time, the penalty might be an extra hour of study time each day for a week. What is even better is if the consequence actually relates to the broken rule.

   I love my friend Barb's description of her punishment when she was using bad language as a rebellious high school freshman. Her mother said, "Daughters who use potty mouth deserve to spend more time in the bathroom. You will be cleaning the bathroom every day for a week or as long as it takes you to clean up your mouth."

2. **The consequence should help improve the child's behavior or eliminate the weakness that caused the problem in the first place.** We need to be very thoughtful about this: grounding a child for lying isn't going to change the child's behavior. Asking the liar to go back to the scene of the crime, however, and tell the truth might help him or her to reconsider telling lies in the future.

3. **The punishment should be realistic.** Don't let your aggravation get the best of you and proclaim an impossible edict that inconveniences everyone else in the family. We should be realistic about how we will supervise the discipline. If it means one parent must be at home to watch a grounded teenager for a month, that is just as much a punishment for the par-

ents as the wayward teenager. Punishments that benefit the entire family, such as cleaning the kitchen, maintaining the yard, or walking the dog, show the offender that disregarding rules affects the community. And, too, the community, the family, witnesses the offender's efforts to take responsibility for the offense. Actions speak loudly.

NEVER RIDICULE OR INTIMIDATE A CHILD

At the heart of all discipline is love: we want those we love to turn around and live righteously. Discipline is never about belittling or diminishing a child's self-esteem. Even in the most treacherous situation, we must be strong enough to uphold the child's image of the self. Calling a child "stupid," "brat," and other names because he or she almost caused a serious accident may relieve our tension but is the last thing a parent should do. Cursing children by calling them a name only increases the damage done. Rather, we need to take a deep breath and explain why the child's action was wrong. If appropriate, explain to the child that what he or she did was a mistake but does not mean that needs to ever happen again.

Craig grew up hearing his dad say to him, "If you had half a brain, you would still be stupid." As an adult, Craig struggles with self-esteem, and his Dad's voice still vibrates in his brain. We owe it to every precious soul that we are forming to nurture that child's spirit with acceptance and love. While discipline can be severe, it should always be administered with mercy and love.

SEVERITY OF DISCIPLINE EQUALS SEVERITY OF THE WRONGDOING

When I was growing up, every infraction required a spanking when Dad got home. Poor Dad! He had no idea what had happened while he was at work. He would walk in the door and immediately be told to spank somebody. Usually I felt so sorry for the poor man that I realized that the spanking hurt him far more than it hurt me. I seemed to know even then that the spanking was not a punishment that had any effect.

Thankfully, the days of such punishment are over. For the most part, we have learned to get creative with punishments that fit the crime. "Time out" is a good example: when a child cannot obey, cannot share, cannot respect authority, and so on, "time out" creates a nonphysical response. Sitting alone to mull over what went wrong is a reasonable consequence. When the culprit, however, is caught red-handed stealing, endangering the life of a playmate, or cheating on a test, for example, we need to up the ante a bit with discipline that fits the crime. It is wise and useful to find a course of punishment that will change the undesirable behavior and teach the severity of the offense.

Colin and his high school freshmen buddies decided to trespass. Not only did they climb on top of the municipal center, they took beer from home and sat on the center's roof drinking it. Of course, they were caught and went to juvenile court. The wise judge gave them a spectacular sentence: every Sunday morning for six weeks, the boys were required to go to the police station and clean the inside of the police cars in which the previous drunk passengers had vomited. Colin learned a powerful lesson about illegal drinking and trespassing. As he cleaned those police cars, he had plenty of time to regret his decision.

EXPLAIN THE DISCIPLINE

There should always be a reasonable relationship between the broken rule and the consequences. Most children and even some of us adults forget just exactly why we are in time-out, paying the fine, being grounded for a month, and so on. Very young children especially forget soon after the crime what it is they did and why they are being punished. In fact, it is best for children to receive the consequences for bad behavior as soon as possible. That's why Dad's spanking appointment with me seemed so senseless. It would have been much more helpful to changing my behavior if my mom had sat with me and talked about why it was wrong to take someone's toy, then told me to give back the toy, and finally told me to spend my time-out thinking of what I could do to be nice to my brother. All of this kind of discipline takes time with and presence to the offender in order to make any impression on a child and to make a difference in behavior. A routine punishment that is always the consequence of the action is much easier on the parent but has little effect on the child.

Taking time to talk about why something was wrong and what the discipline is all about means that we have to put aside our own agenda for the needs of our child. In a busy household with much to do, we often choose what is easier rather than what is best. What I know from experience disciplining teens and young adults is that they are more than willing to obey a rule if they understand why it exists. They will cooperate with the discipline as long as they understand why they are being punished. Gone are the days when saying "because I said so" and "never mind your sports schedule, mister, you are grounded" was effective.

Mark and Sally were at the end of their rope regarding their young son Evan's behavior. Since baby sister Evelyn was born, Evan craved attention and decided to get that attention by breaking every family rule he could. He broke lamps from tossing baseballs in the living room, he spilled milk purposefully during meals, and he even resorted to wetting his bed at night. It wasn't until Sally had a long talk with Evan's pediatrician that she realized what was going on. As a consequence of that chat, Sally and Mark began to spend more one-on-one time with Evan, letting him know that he didn't have to do bad things to be noticed by them. Evan still bore discipline when he acted out, but now those punishments were explained, and special time to discuss Evan's feelings was included in his time-outs. Soon life in their household calmed down.

CRITICIZE IN PRIVATE

The last bit of wisdom about discipline is something everyone knows already but still needs to hear: we should never humiliate a child in a public setting. Criticism and correction need to be delivered at a private time—parent and child only. When we correct a child in front of others, the child is usually so concerned about being called out in public and being embarrassed that what we say never gets through to the child. If you find yourself outside the home and it is necessary to discipline a child, find a corner or go to the car or leave the gym for a moment for a focused discussion.

When we discipline our children, we offer them a grace. So many parents refrain from holding a firm disciplinary line because they want to do the loving thing. Yet, if love is sure and full of mercy, it can be that when we hold children accountable and teach them the ways of what is right and good, we love them with a kind of love that is harder on us than on them. The long-term effects of good discipline allow children to know that their parents love them in spite of their failings. It is gentle assurance and mercy that temper every act of correction. It is this lesson that will stand the test of time. One of the most difficult tasks of parenting is teaching a child that what they do has consequences. The world will not excuse them, and we must prepare them to live in that world.

Remember

- Establish with your child an understanding of rules and their consequences as your firm yet loving method of discipline. Everyone in your family needs to be on board about what constitutes acceptable behavior and what violates the rule.

- Administer consequences with your heart as well as with your head: the punishment should fit the crime; the consequence should help improve your child's behavior or eliminate the weakness that caused the problem in the first place; and the punishment should be realistic.

- Nurture your child's spirit with acceptance and love, and discipline your child with mercy and love.

- Find a course of punishment that will change your child's undesirable behavior and teach the severity of the offense.

- Take time to talk with your child about why something was wrong and what the discipline is all about.

- Criticize and correct your child's behavior in private, never in public.

Ponder

1. What is a consequence or punishment that you still remember from your childhood?

2. What are three of your family rules?

3. Why do you think parents choose name-calling, ridicule, and inappropriate punishments when their child breaks a rule?

4. What can you do when you witness a child being abused by an adult?

Exercise

Meet soon with your family members to create ten commandments for your family. Let each person write his or her own list. By consensus create the final list and then decide on appropriate discipline for breaking a commandment. Post the family's ten commandments on the refrigerator and keep everyone accountable.

Pray

O God of Light, teach me to see that what I choose
    has consequences.
When I choose what is good, right, and perfect, I
    am formed in your image.

Likewise, when I sin, my spirit knows a darkness
    that is not from you.
I ask that I might magnify your presence in all that I do,
    and when I fail to obey you, I ask you to bring me
    back to your sacred heart with mercy. Amen.

CHAPTER 6

Morality Happens in Groups

If it were possible to isolate ourselves into a protected, regulated environment in which we could control behavior and distance ourselves from those who were immoral, all our problems would be solved. Unfortunately, utopia is a myth, and God seems to encourage us to rub elbows with all sorts of sheep—black and white and gray.

It is in the arena of real life that children begin to understand the challenge of choosing to uphold a righteous way of living. The Gospel is full of characters who illustrate this: the good Samaritan preceded by two guys who had no time for the beaten man, the little boy present at the miracle of the loaves and fishes in the midst of a crowd of people who did not choose to share their lunch, the poor woman who chose to give her only coins to others.

As parents we are required to offer our children the fine skill of comparing and contrasting those who choose good with those who do not. Without this knowledge, our children are formed in a naive world and have no real idea of the depth of darkness that just waits to snatch them. The devil does seem to go about as a roaring lion looking for someone to devour, and it is our job to make absolutely sure it is not our child who is devoured.

SUPERVISE MEDIA

The most obvious place to start in guiding a child's conscience is with electronic media. Our families are bombarded each day with an unfiltered, huge quantity of information, entertainment, and education that enters our home with the click of a button, mouse, or switch. The culture reflected in this media is often far from the moral ideal that we would like to offer to our children. Sexual promiscuity, marital infidelity, murder, stealing, gossip, and more are promoted as acceptable—and sometimes even as desirable. The Ten Commandments seem obsolete in our society due to the encouragement of a philosophy that says, "If it pleases you, it is good." Yet, there are other little bastions of light in the mix. Public television with its quality programs, websites that promote moral goodness, and books and movies that tell modern parables can be found when you seek them.

As parents our job is to strictly monitor what media is allowed in our homes. The computer, tablets, smartphones, music players, Netflix, social media such as Facebook and

Twitter, cell phone texts, handheld video games, and so much more must be kept on our radar. This is terribly difficult when many such devices are very portable and easily hidden. We must supervise young children all the time when they are exposed to media. Older children need to understand why we limit their use of electronic media, and we must work constantly with them to build a relationship of trust of and respect for our judgment as gatekeepers to electronic content and its influences. When possible, for instance, parents should block unwanted websites and TV channels and then explain objections for viewing and accessing to the child. And, too, parents should track their child's texting and phone usage and discuss the number of texts and calls when the phone bill arrives each month. Parents should at a minimum read online or print reviews of movies their children want to watch.

Kim was horrified when she checked her fourteen-year-old son Joey's recent website history. She discovered that Joey had been surfing pornographic sites, and her heart broke. How could her precious boy be poisoning his mind (and soul) with this filth? I reassured her that all was not lost. Joey was a normal, curious teenager. Rather than accuse him in a rage, I advised her to see this event as a teaching moment to explain to him the danger and evil of pornography and how it exploits others. I told Kim to do everything in her power to keep the lines of communication open with her son and to tell him that if he has more questions about this issue or any others he discovers on the Internet, she was happy to talk. Then I told her to move Joey's computer out of his room and into a common space in their home. I encouraged her to monitor other avenues as well: phone messages, texting, and any doors that could lead

Joey into trouble. This situation typifies the kind of vigilance required of parents in this age of electronic media.

STAY ON TOP OF EDUCATION

Home schooling has become very popular in the last decades. When I ask why parents choose staying home with their children to educate them, one of the primary reasons I hear is to control what information their child receives. The home-schooling parents have an educational philosophy that they are passionate about: they want to offer their child a system of education that filters out ideas they find objectionable and filters in those ideas that may not be included in the public school program. The most important of these ideas are morality and spirituality. The home schoolers work hard at holding up role models of decency, patriotism, political justice, and so on. While this is not the only reason families choose home schooling, it certainly is an essential element.

What about the rest of us? Many of us trust our children's educations to private and public schools. When a child enters the educational system, it is not the time in a child's life, or in the life of the family for that matter, to trust blindly. It is important for parents to become involved in their children's schools by joining educational organizations, reviewing children's textbooks, visiting online school websites, and communicating with other parents and the faculty about what is being taught. It is also very important to open a child's book bag and then ask the child to explain the contents. Not only is this an excellent opportunity to stay informed of the child's progress, it gives the parent a chance to find out what is going on in the classroom from the child's perspective.

One of my sons was not a great reporter of what was happening at his school. His mind was absorbed with sports. When I asked him how things were going at school, I got "Fine." When I asked what he was doing in science class, the answer was "Nothing." I then came upon a solution that broke through this communication barrier: our neighbor's daughter, Clare, was in his class. Clare was a very bright and friendly little girl so I asked her to answer the same questions I asked my son. I was amazed at what I heard. Not only did Clare tell me all the wonderful lessons at school, she shared stories about my son's success in those classes. While at times I felt like I was spying on my boy, I was reassured that all was well in the fourth grade. I shared these stories with Clare's parents so that they too were informed. Communication goes beyond property lines!

SUNDAY NIGHT FAMILY SUPPERS

Years ago I read about the Kennedy family and John Kennedy's experience of the family supper table. It was at these evening meals that Joe Kennedy, the father of this clan, held court. He talked about world affairs, quizzed the children on their opinions, reviewed history with them, and in general held open discussions of what was going on in the world of politics, religion, and science. John Kennedy later said that this experience at the family supper table was instrumental in forming his mind and conscience.

Our own family supper table can hold the same promise. A great way to use the family group dynamic is at the table where everyone seems pleased to be there—after all, everyone must eat! A tasty meal encourages discussion and conversation that is relaxed and spontaneous. It is here that an informal discussion on moral choices, situation ethics, and opinions about current events can occur without sounding like a parental lecture. In this safe and affirming setting, children can share what is happening in their lives, and other family members can offer advice and support. The addition of guests to the family table can enliven and enrich conversation and open up new perspectives on an issue or situation.

A weekly Sunday supper (or another day of the week that is convenient to everyone) should be a required date for everyone in the family. I love to serve these meals at the dining room table with a little extra attention to table setting and the menu so that the family knows that this is a special meal and worth looking forward to. At such occasions, the Kennedy family agenda works so well: ask each family member to share what their week was like and any successes they experienced; listen for topics that lend themselves to discussions of doing the right thing; ask open-ended questions to elicit opinions and new perspectives.

In this group setting we begin to understand the diversity of opinions and to defend those opinions with people who love us. When we sit in friendly territory, the skill of debate can be fostered, and we can raise children who have moral principles that they can defend. I began Sunday suppers when my children were in grade school. Now that my children are young, independent adults with families of their own, Sunday supper together is still a priority for all of us. These suppers became and continue to be an arena for ideas and truth.

MAKE ONE-ON-ONE TIME

While groups provide an important aid in forming a moral child, there is one group that is essential to raising a moral child: the "group" that is just you and your child. Being alone with your child for one-on-one time allows a special bond to form that should always be encouraged and allowed to develop, despite any tension between parent and child. Being alone with your child is a secure time when parent and child meet and anything can be said without condemnation and when loving support and advice is always available. In the safety of a conversation with a parent, the deepest and most difficult questions can be broached.

If this is not the case in a relationship with a son or daughter, it is never too late for a parent to begin. A parent can start by scheduling one-on-one time with each child, deciding with each child what the agenda will be and where parent and child will come together. Parents and children might feel most comfortable viewing a movie together and eating pizza afterwards, or attending a sporting event to sit side by side and talk about anything. The most important factors in choosing one-on-one time with a child are to ensure that the venue or activity is something the child will enjoy and that there is adequate time to talk about what's going on in the child's life and the parent's.

When my friend Rob divorced and remarried, his new wife suggested that he and his teenaged daughter Denise meet weekly for dinner out so that the two of them could catch up and have some meaningful father-daughter talk. As Denise matured and married and had children of her own, Rob continued the practice and worked around Denise's schedule.

This one-on-one time is a time to listen to a child and not succumb to the desire to lecture a child on what to do and what not to do. The quickest turnoff for an adolescent or young adult is to be told by a parent exactly what needs to be done, where the teen or young adult went wrong, how to not make the same mistake again, and so on. If the child asks those questions, the parent should respond but wait for the child to make the first move. It is also important at such times to affirm the child by pointing out the good in that child as well as the parent's faith and trust in the child and the desire to stand by the child in his or her daily life choices.

What does a parent do if a child gives the silent treatment? I suggest asking questions that do not have definite single-word answers. Rather than asking "How's school going?" to which the predictable answer is "Fine," ask, "What happened to that science project you were working on?" or "I saw that amazing drawing you were working on. Have you thought about getting involved in the art competition?" When the child responds, return the volley with more questions.

One day Brittney, 15, came home from school crying and unwilling to talk about whatever was bothering her. Her mom, Missy, said nothing about the tears and then scheduled pedicures for both her and Brittney. As the mother and daughter relaxed in the salon, Brittney opened up and revealed that several girls in the school show choir had begun bullying her. Missy was able to offer some strategies for dealing with bullies and also to affirm her daughter's intelligence and beauty and innate goodness. Missy made a note to contact the school counselor so that she and Brittney could report and discuss what happened. Waiting until Brittney was ready to talk and was relaxed made all the difference in how Missy reacted to the situation.

One of the best places to start the conversation ball rolling is in a car going to and from school or sports events or while running errands. My brood of children included two introverts who were not easily prompted into talking about anything with their mother. Strangely, I noticed a trend beginning: our best heart-to-heart conversations seemed to happen in the car when we were both staring ahead and there was no uncomfortable face-to-face probing, the doors were locked, and we were driving sixty miles per hour down the highway, which prevented any escape from interaction. I remember well the time in the car when one son asked me, "Mom, how do you know when you love a girl?"

SHARE THE WORLD OUTSIDE HOME

Earlier I mentioned the negative effect of isolating our children. Now I want to explore what is positive about exposing children to this wonderful world. The natural world is full of opportunities for life lessons about cause and effect, lessons that help parents drive home that what we choose to do causes consequences.

Ecology, conservation, weather patterns, agriculture, and horticulture can become additional and vital resources in identifying life's boundaries and consequences, not to mention the awesome spectacle of the Creator's handiwork when we become aware of the divine source of life and the breathtaking beauty of God's touch. We should include frequent trips to natural sites and outdoor activities to reinforce the lessons that experiencing beauty and nature can affect our life choices: a hike in the woods on a crisp autumn day can provide calm to a stressed spirit, making snow angels during a snowstorm can spark play and bring simple joy, planting bulbs for next year's spring and summer bloom can teach about planning, and canoeing with buddies on a summer day can teach teamwork and how to get along with others.

The world is also the place to teach the lessons of justice and diversity. Spending time with a child to watch the evening news and talk about the injustice—and sometimes even the justice!—we see is an excellent way to expose our children to "man's inhumanity to man" and how the world needs compassion and righteous voices and hands everywhere. These newscasts then become moments to point out just and unjust actions that cause pain and misery to thousands each day, as well as witness to people helping others in profound ways.

My friend, Lisa, a grandmother of two, bought a large world map, affixed it to poster board, and hung the map in the family TV room so that during newscasts she could identify for her grandchildren the location mentioned on the news. Not only does the map help her grandkids learn geography, it helps them become more aware that there is a world beyond their backyard and that it is our duty and privilege to learn and care about people around the globe.

The news is also where we witness how some people break the moral law. When a child hears on the news about thefts, assaults, murders, genocide, political corruption, war, and so on, parents can provide commentary and point out who broke the moral law, why it was wrong to do so, and who was hurt as a result of the law breaker's actions.

There is, thankfully, also good news to observe on TV. One family in Oregon created a "good news" site on a kitchen blackboard/bulletin board: whenever a family member found an item in the newspaper or heard about a person who did the right thing, he or she noted the good news on the board. At each month's end the board was purged of good news items so that completely new good news items could be listed. The Oregon parents remarked that their three children soon became keen observers of what is good about others, and the delightful consequence was that the three children's behavior improved dramatically.

Another valuable lesson in taking our children into the world is to teach them the lesson of diversity—to see that what we believe to be the right way is not the only way. Learning that everyone is not like us creates an awareness of how others perceive our actions. Helping our child sort out absolute moral good from those choices that are different but both morally good will test our own knowledge of what is good. Many a philosopher has struggled with this question. For instance, a Hindu mother and a Christian mother may have different versions of modest dress, so we teach our child that both mothers honor their moral belief, and both are good. That lesson can only happen in a world in which our children learn to honor diversity. An added bonus in this endeavor is that more often than not our children become our teachers. Our preconceived biases fade in the light of a child's perspective.

We cannot protect our children from the outside world nor should we want to protect them. Morality happens in the wider realm of family, school, media, sports, politics, and hundreds of other sources of human beings creating different versions of the good life. What is required of us is to give our children the discernment to discover these differences without fear. Children must stand strong as they encounter life outside the protection of their home and grow to adulthood with a love for others and the courage to hold strong to their own moral code. Our hope is that our children learn from us that this larger arena is a place of acceptance and open mindedness.

Remember

- Monitor strictly what media you will allow in your home and identify for your child what content he or she can access. Also, establish and explain the consequences for disregarding the family's media usage rules.

- Become involved in your child's schooling by joining educational organizations, reviewing your child's textbooks, visiting online school websites, communicating with other parents and the faculty about what is being taught, and so on.

- Schedule Sunday supper (or some other day convenient to all family members) and make participation mandatory with few exceptions. This venue allows you and your child and guests to express opinions in a safe and loving circle, to respond to open-ended questions, and to invite discussion and exploration of moral issues.

- Share with your child the world outside the home (whether the natural world or the world found on the TV evening newscast) as a resource and aid for reinforcing moral lessons and consequences.

Ponder

1. What do you believe to be the most threatening immoral influences for your child?

2. How are you involved in your child's education? What are additional ways to be involved?

3. What moral issue do you find difficult to discuss with others? Why?

4. What are some of your favorite family table memories?

5. Discuss some situations when moral good is absolute. When is there more than one moral response to an ethical situation, for example, dress, tithing, government funding?

Exercise

Host a family supper for your family or your extended family. Think about starting this tradition each month as a forum for a moral discussion. Enlist your child in planning and hosting the supper and identifying possible topics.

Pray

God of all people, lead me into the circle of life.
Break the barriers in my family that keep us from
    talking honestly about what we think and feel.
Give me the courage to reach out to those with whom I
    disagree, the strength to stand up for what I believe,
    and the compassion to understand those who reject
    my beliefs. Amen.

CHAPTER 7

Fashioning a Moral Code

As parents of two children, Tim and Michelle decided early in their parenthood that they wanted their children to grow up helping others and to be generous when others needed help. So Michelle and Tim decided to sponsor an annual yard sale with the proceeds from the sale to benefit local charities. The parents challenged their children to collect items for the sale, tag the items with prices, and staff the sale on a summer Saturday. After many hours of canvassing the neighborhood and family members for used household items and clothing, the children scheduled a day for the sale, made signs to put on the main road near their home, and then organized and displayed the items. The children enlisted the help of other neighbor children to work the sale and promote it. All the children dressed in colorful costumes and took turns going to the main road, waving wildly and cheerily to direct drivers to the sale.

Michelle and Tim had instructed their children to designate the charities to which the sale profits would go and so the children made a sign to inform customers about the charities for that year. In the first year of the annual yard sale, the children netted over six hundred dollars; in the second year they set a higher goal and netted nearly eight hundred dollars; in the third year the net was one thousand dollars. Each year, after cleaning up the yard and stowing leftover sale items, the children delivered the yard sale proceeds personally to the charity. One year, the children designated a church food pantry as their charity of choice, and they called the pantry director to inquire about what food items were needed and then went shopping for those items and later delivered them to the pantry director. Tim and Michelle willingly drove their children to deliver the sale proceeds and then treated their children to a special lunch.

By modeling compassionate behavior to their children and even the neighborhood children, Tim and Michelle had fulfilled a primary task of every parent: to pass on to their children a moral code. This moral code—a collection of values, traditions, and beliefs that influence what we consider right and true—is a personal decision. Every family, every culture, and every individual can and should create a unique collection of factors that influence what they consider good, right, and perfect. This moral code affects what we determine to be right or wrong. We need the wisdom of the ages that comes from our parents, our neighbors, our teachers, our spiritual guides, our church, our society. We need to be carefully taught.

Somehow, however, some parents presume that passing on to their children what they believe will "just happen." Sadly, this is not true. We have all witnessed children and adults who cannot seem to determine right from wrong and do not have a clue how to act or think when a situation arises that demands a moral choice. Most likely, such folks are the product of a family that did not teach and model a code of moral behavior. In such circumstances and left to their own instincts, some people develop a moral code that is piecemeal and not always grounded in wisdom. "It just feels right" becomes their mantra when making moral choices.

A more pressing issue, however, remains: What *is* our particular moral code? Have we ever taken time to think about it? How do the rules, laws, and behaviors, and so on, that are a part of what we believe and are sacred to us impact our daily decisions? Are these rules of behavior something we want to pass on to those who come after us? Many times I interact with parents who realize that their adult child has no sense of the laws and directives that they as parents hold sacred. These parents have not been intentional in passing on their personal moral code.

How do we communicate this moral code to our children without giving the Moral Code 101 lecture and turning off our children? Here are some subtle ways borrowed from a previous generation to get the moral code message across.

NOTE PEOPLE WE ADMIRE AND WHY

Many ways exist to share our beliefs with our children. A wise place to begin is by noting to a child other people whom we admire and then sharing stories of those who led heroic lives, holy lives, inspiring lives. Everyone loves an inspiring story.

When children get lost in the drama and imaginary journey of a saint, war hero, famous inventor, or an outstanding leader of change, they begin to relate to morality in a real-life situation. Joshua Lawrence Chamberlain is a perfect example. This U.S. Civil War Union army commander won the battle of Little Round Top at Gettysburg against all odds. His famous command, "Forward, at all cost forward," was an act of bravery that still inspires anyone who faces insurmountable obstacles. I love to sit on Little Round Top and listen to parents tell their sons and daughters Chamberlain's story. Recently, when visiting Gettysburg, I overheard a young boy ask his dad, "Can real people do things like that?" His father's answer was priceless: "Son, you will do this and even greater things if you have courage."

Such is the power of inspirational stories to teach. Parents should seek these stories everywhere, but especially from the media because children look to the media for authority and credibility. Books, social media, movies, and television can be valuable resources for parents because they offer inspiring stories that have the potential to create magic moments with a child. Media can influence in ways that Grandpa's story of the world war can never compete. Of course, when possible, such media resources should be reviewed and filtered first by parents.

LIVE LIFE THE WAY YOU WANT A CHILD TO LIVE

The tendency of some parents is to give a child lessons: tennis lessons, computer lessons, swim lessons, music lessons, and, at times, even faith lessons. We pay a fee and someone teaches our child how to play tennis, use the computer, swim like a fish, play a musical instrument with competency, and believe in God. In order to afford all these lessons a parent may work extra hours thus giving up the time that could have been spent with a child to teach the same things.

In an ideal world, every family could choose to put quality time as a first priority, but we all know that life is far from the ideal. A good friend of mine, Kim, is a single mom whose husband died of cancer two years ago. Kim has four beautiful daughters. In order to make enough money to pay the bills, Kim works two jobs and cleans houses at night. Kim's girls don't get a lot of time with their mother in these hard times. We know many others in Kim's shoes. We can offer our resources and time to provide those who have no choice more time with their children. There is no better charitable donation than the donation of time to a family without a minute to spare.

Time spent sharing our enthusiasm and skill for any endeavor impacts a child's soul as well as body and mind. Little ones want to grow up to be just like Mommy and Daddy. I often tell parents who come to the first parent meeting for religious education, "No catechism, no pastor, no teacher can bring your child to faith. Your child will be exactly the kind of Christian that you are."

When we think deeply about our own passions, we realize that many things that we love came from people who taught us to love the same things. My friend, Louise, tells me often that her love of the domestic arts—cooking, gardening, home decorating, entertaining—comes from observing and helping her mother, grandmothers, and two aunts—all of whom excelled at making their homes oases of happiness and beauty.

Father Robert Barron, one of today's great spiritual teachers, tells the story of his father taking him to baseball games. He says that from the time he was a small boy his father and he went to the games and cheered with thousands of fans. At home his father taught him to catch and bat. Robert dreamed of becoming a professional baseball player. All through his youth he and his father grew in their passion for the game. Then Father Barron dropped the bomb to his listener: what if parents applied the same passion for baseball (or whatever) to passion for God? Our churches, he says, would be full, and every family would place their faith at the center of everyday life. Father Barron's point is that we become the same people that our parents are. If we are devoted to making money, to having expensive things, and to being a professional success, we will pass on those same values to our children who will devote their lives too to putting those things first. Taken a step further, our passion will influence what we believe to be morally right.

We must always be aware that our children are always watching us. While the words we say will have some influence on our child, our actions will have even greater influence. If children see us lying, cheating, losing our temper, abusing substances and other people, and so on, they will come to embrace those same behaviors as acceptable and even as desirable.

The good things we do and the moral way we act carry the same power as the destructive and immoral things we do. I witnessed this with Brianna, who helped her Grandma bake pies every Saturday morning. Each week Anna Brewster and little Brianna baked a different kind of pie. At the end of each baking session, Brianna took home one pie, Grandma kept one pie, and the third pie was given to someone needy, perhaps a neighbor grieving the loss of her husband, or a new family just registered at church, or a single parent with little money for pie. The last time I spoke with Anna she told me that Brianna was training as a pastry chef and volunteering at an inner-city soup kitchen. Brianna is growing up in Grandma's image and living a moral code of generosity and service passed on to her from Grandma.

TEACH A CHILD TO PROTECT THE INNOCENT AND VULNERABLE

People like to describe our world as "dog eat dog" with its hit-and-run traffic accidents, elderly homeless dying in trash heaps, millionaires cheating retirees out of their life savings because of greed, and on and on. These are not pretty pictures. And every day we learn of another injustice, another immoral choice based on someone's selfish love.

At the core of every Christian's moral code is Jesus' mandate to love others as we love ourselves. The Gospel has no place for absolute, self-centered narcissism. Contrary to popular opinion, it really isn't "all about me." The moral code we fashion needs to keep in mind that caring for the innocent and vulnerable is part of our very fiber.

Somewhere in the early years of a child's life, we begin to show the child the way to real happiness. We experience that in giving of ourselves to others who need us and finding contentment and even delight in doing so. We cannot explain this to our children; we must simply invite them into the experience. It would be a very valuable lesson to reach out to others as a family a few times each year by *together* working in a soup kitchen, visiting a nursing home, cleaning a neighbor's garage, babysitting for a newborn to give a tired parent a few hours of rest, or whatever comes your way to teach this wordless lesson of protecting the innocent and vulnerable.

POINT OUT COMPASSIONATE BEHAVIOR

While it is great to roll up our sleeves and serve others, we can also just watch other people rise to the call. We learn about doing acts of service and kindness by pointing out others who've done kind things for us. I suspect most of us just take for granted all the quiet acts of service that occur around us each day.

My children refer affectionately to the invisible presence that cleans the house, washes dishes, and does the laundry as the "house fairy." The house fairy is the person who washes the jeans a daughter doesn't want cleaned because they might shrink, who bakes chocolate chip cookies while others are at work, and who vacuums Dad's car when he sleeps in one Saturday. Our house fairy is one among us who chooses to perform acts of love because it is rewarding like nothing else she could do.

A few years ago, I shared a story at a retreat I was giving for a high school faculty. I told the teachers of a Lenten day when I was doing a "random act of kindness" while in line at the drive-thru window of a fast food restaurant. Using the rearview mirror, I looked at the car behind me. It was filled with twelve-year-old boy soccer players. At the wheel was a harried mom. I drove up to the window and asked to pay for the order that woman had just placed. I drove away with my diet cola and sandwich feeling sneaky and delighted. About a week after that retreat, I received a thank-you from the faculty. Inside the envelope was a fifty-dollar gift card for that restaurant. The teachers told me to enjoy a few more sandwiches on them. It seems that compassion comes back to us.

We want our children to learn this lesson. Becoming a compassionate human being brings meaning to our moral code. We come to understand that caring about others affords blessing to everyone and is the good and right thing to do.

EXPLAIN VALUES

The moral code needs more than a listing of the concepts involved. We need to explain to our children the reason *why* these precepts are important to us. The Millennial generation is not made up of "yes" men and women. These young adults want to understand the *reason* we think and do things. What impresses me about the Millennials is that they require each of us to be thoughtful and to examine just why patriotism or social justice is right. For many of us from older generations, this requires rethinking our stand.

I raised my four children not to be quitters. Quitting, I believe, shows a certain lack of character and doing so just because things get hard or are inconvenient is a sign of weakness. As a result, in our family, if you joined a sports team, you played the entire season regardless of how good or bad the team performed. Quitting is not an option.

I didn't think I needed to explain this value until my youngest son was benched by his varsity soccer coach. Chris was an all-state athlete, but there was bad chemistry between him and the coach. Each week my boy sat on the bench. The team lost more often than they won. My son felt frustrated and angry that he was not allowed to contribute. It was after another loss that my son told me he wanted to quit the team. We sat in the high school parking lot and talked out this dilemma. I realized that I had never really explained why quitting was against my standards. It wasn't that it was morally wrong or right; it was that I believe we need to be true to our word, that we need to be determined and strong in every situation. If we quit in small things, how will we act when our marriage is in trouble or when our church fails us? I told my son that the soccer team was a testing ground for his fortitude and that sitting on that bench would build character. I told him that I was more proud of his bench sitting than if he had scored a hundred goals. He finished that season in dismal defeat, but he learned a lot about human nature and what it takes to put up with someone who rejects you.

In order to explain our moral code to our children, we, as parents, must give some thought to the *reason* we practice our moral code. It is invaluable to know what is important to us and why. Frugal people need to examine why frugality is vital to them. Patriotic people must work through their love of country from more than a level of "America, love it or leave it." Religious people must come to understand why faith makes a difference to them.

Fashioning and passing on our moral code requires that we know what we hold dear. It means too that we act purposefully about our passions. If what we hold dear as our moral code is never witnessed or expressed in action, if those things in which we believe never motivate us to act on them, then this moral code stands as an empty promise. Our children will not so much remember what we said but what we did.

Remember

- Examine your moral code from the unique collection of factors that influences what you consider good, right, and perfect. This moral code affects what you determine to be right or wrong.

- Note to your child other people whom you admire and then share stories of those who you think led heroic lives, holy lives, inspiring lives.

- Live your life the way you want your child to live. How you act, even more than what you say, will influence your child's behavior.

- Give yourself to others who need you and find contentment and even delight in doing so.

- Explain to your child the reasons why your moral code is important to you.

Ponder

1. How would you describe the term "moral code" to your child?

2. In what way has a book or film influenced your moral code?

3. What are some values expressed in your moral code (for example, "never put off until tomorrow what you can do today," "God and country first," "use what you have before buying more")?

4. Who do you admire for his or her strong moral code?

5. What lesson about moral standards have you learned from your family?

Exercise

List three beliefs or practices you hold sacred. Then write a brief statement about why each practice is important in your life. Then share these three beliefs or practices with your child.

Pray

Spirit of Wisdom, allow me to carry in my heart
  your law.
May I begin to know your divine voice deep within
  my being that teaches me the way of truth and
  good.
Give me the sure knowledge of your way and direct me
  in ways everlasting. Amen.

CHAPTER 8

Be Fair

"Fair" is a very good way to understand justice. Most of us shy away from terms like "social justice" that can imply radical behavior such as standing in front of an abortion clinic with signs, taking part in sit-ins at courthouses, and organizing protest marches, and so on. We like our justice watered down so that we don't have to consider actually standing up for what is right.

But, in reality, the term "justice" simply means being fair, giving what is right to those who are being denied what is good. When I speak about justice, I always begin by tackling fairness first. When we understand the concept of being fair, then understanding and practicing justice is just an easy step forward.

It is the same for our children. We can begin to teach them justice by pointing out how and when to do what is fair. Then, the concept of making just decisions comes easier.

Think about the ways in which we have experienced fairness. In sports, a baseball is fair or foul. Fair balls are in the arena of play, while a foul ball has left the field of play and no runner can score runs. When someone cheats at games, we will say, "That wasn't fair." We mean that the actions were not within the accepted boundaries. So it is with teaching fairness to our children. We are teaching them what is acceptable, right, and good.

Fairness also implies that we are willing to care about how our actions can hurt others. Fairness requires that everyone get a "fair shake" or equal benefit. This may sound so rudimentary. Yet, children do not understand justice without learning it from us. Ask any preschool teacher about discipline of her children. She will say that they need to be taught to share, listen, and follow instructions. These little ones learn the lesson of fairness by seeing it played out among their peers. In a like way at home, it will not be our words that teach fairness but our actions before our children.

KNOW YOUR OWN BIAS

Like it or not, we pass on to our children our attitudes about politics, religion, finance, lifestyle, and so many other things that didn't even seem significant at the time. We find ourselves repeating phrases our mother used, buying the same kind of car Dad bought, and even choosing mustard or catsup for our hot dog. Little ones worship their parents. They want to be just like them. They grow up to instinctively repeat the actions and words of their parents. So it comes as no surprise that they will absorb not only our good side but our faults as well.

We must be aware that our children will inherit our personal bias against any group or ideology. Usually during late adolescence our children seem to reject everything parents hold sacred and then these teens and young adults reclaim some of the sacred treasures as their own. One psychologist told me that it is as if the farmer's son and daughter empty the barn of all the animals. When the barn is empty, the farmer's child peruses the barnyard and invites back into the barn the animals they have chosen to live on their farm. During this time of rebellion, it is so important that parents are able to defend what we hold sacred. It is also a time when our silent resentments, personal biases, and prejudices become apparent. It can be a rude awakening to see that we cannot defend a sacred treasure because, in truth, it is a bias that is unjust. Our children become our greatest teachers.

Kara tells the story of her sixteen-year-old daughter who asked her if it was okay for her to date boys of other races. What shocked Kara was her quick response to her daughter, "I don't care what race your boyfriends are, as long as they are Catholic." It was eye-opening for Kara to realize that she was perfectly comfortable with racial diversity but fiercely biased against people of other religions. As Kara looked back on her example of religious intolerance, she was shocked to realize that she had spoken loud and clear that only Catholics were welcome in the family social circle. It was a subtle bias that influenced Kara's entire family.

Many Catholic families embrace interfaith marriage in their ranks. The Catholic Church honors interfaith unions as blessed and holy. It is a terribly unjust bias that would allow anyone to think that these marriages are any less holy and grace-filled than a sacrament between two Catholics. While an interfaith marriage has many unique challenges, they, too, prosper when the husband and wife work together with God in their holy union.

The sooner we realize our own bias, the easier it will be for us to keep from making decisions and judgments that reinforce our feelings and affect our child. Often, we simply have adopted the bias of our own parents, and then the bias cycle continues in the next generations. It is the situation of the feuding Hatfields and McCoys at its worst.

TALK ABOUT SOCIETY'S PREJUDICES AND FAIRNESS

The easiest way to hold a forum on society's unjust practices is to talk about every example that comes into our daily lives. From early childhood into adulthood, we can teach our children to analyze the news of the day. When a child reports an incident at school that required discipline, parents should explain for the child the reason for the discipline. When a referee makes a bad call that allows the opponent to win, parents should talk about the call. It will not be the great injustices that streak across the evening television news that alone teach the lesson of human's inhumanity to human, but the times when injustice touches us personally.

The immorality of abortion was all theory until the junior class at the local high school was asked to support a classmate who was choosing to have a baby rather than abort. The class was asked to include the young mother-to-be in their social lives, to provide baby supplies, to stand by their classmate academically so that she could keep up with her studies. It made a difference for that circle of students who stood by their pregnant friend. When the baby was delivered and placed in the mother's arms, that small band of supporters was allowed to be with her. The joy of the moment and the deep conviction that life is real and precious from the moment of conception was branded on each of their consciences.

While the national, world, and local news may not always touch home, it is still vital that we keep our children abreast of the headlines. What becomes a challenge is finding unbiased reports of this news. The Democrats are favored on one channel, and the Republicans hold court on another. Our Christian values are condemned as archaic by those who support premarital sex and right-to-life issues. Thus, it is important that we monitor and mentor the news with our children. As a parent myself, I have found repeatedly that explaining the worldview to my children necessitated that I think about my own moral platform as it impacted these national and world events. Sometimes, when we must put our thoughts in understandable language for a child, we discover the real truth of the matter for ourselves.

NEVER LET A BIGOTED STATEMENT GO UNCHALLENGED

The real test of how well we have established a moral platform for a child is when they witness an incident or hear words that betray another's bigotry. We cannot, in fact, we must not, allow such statements to slide by. Ignoring them validates them. We must stop what we are doing at the very moment bigotry occurs and point it out to our child and clearly define it as grossly wrong.

This is not the easiest thing to do. In fact, more often than not, our first tendency is to ignore someone's cruel remarks because we don't want to cause a problem. It is hard to muster up the courage to stand up for what we believe when it will open us up to persecution or ridicule. A saying that I hold dear is "Do what you teach, or else you are teaching something else." In this situation that "something else" is bigotry. Inadvertently, every time we stand silently by and allow a racial slur or belittling comment to go by, we are teaching our child that this bigotry is acceptable.

Name-calling seems to be the first place bigotry rears its ugly head. Children just seem to learn at an early age how to tear someone apart by calling the person a derogatory name. Recently, Julia's three-year-old daughter, Lindsey, was sitting in her car seat while her mom drove through rush-hour traffic. Someone cut off mom in traffic, and, without thinking, mom spoke a racial slur. The next day at day care Lindsey repeated that name when another toddler took her toy. The unacceptable behavior was reported to mom when she picked up Lindsey that evening. Julia told me she was completely mortified when she realized she had taught her child that ancient art of name-calling. Mom swallowed her pride and explained that mommy made a horrible mistake and that it was a bad name.

But, the damage was done. The deeper lesson Lindsey learned from mom that day was that when we are angry at someone, we can hurt them by saying something hateful about their appearance, their race, their intelligence, and so on. When we translate this toddler lesson into adult behavior, it wreaks havoc throughout our life with relationships and communal peace.

Human nature just seems to enjoy the "we vs. they" syndrome: the desire to be the best ones, the good ones, the smart ones. In order for us to be all those things, some others must become the worst, the bad, and the dumbest ones. It is simply a human need to possess a misplaced power over others that leads us to this kind of immorality. African tribes have been at war for centuries because of their differences. There are still places in this country that hold a grudge that began with the Civil War. Not long ago, I was taken back and curiously surprised when I was speaking in Louisiana and was introduced as "that Yankee woman"! I had never thought of myself as a Yankee. I live in Ohio. Yet in the deep South anyone north of the Mason-Dixon line is on the Yankee list.

As parents, teachers, and role models for the young, we must guard our tongues and our actions lest they betray any remnant of bigotry. When our children hear or witness these things, it is time to sit down and talk about what an evil it is to believe that anyone is better than another because of their race, religion, or culture.

READ AND TALK ABOUT DIVERSITY

How do we teach our children well concerning diversity? A lecture doesn't work. It seems that real-life observation has much more grace.

When I was working in a grade school a few years back, we had a terrible problem with the first-grade girls. A group of young Caucasian girls had shunned Sadie, an African American girl. Sadie had no friends, no one would play with her, no one would eat lunch with her, and so on. She went home every day in tears. The principal asked me to hold an intervention. So I gathered the girls and asked them why they wouldn't play with Sadie. They knew they had done something wrong but couldn't quite understand what was wrong with wanting to be with people like themselves. They saw Sadie as an outsider because she had brown skin. Amid all their tears, I explained that white skin and brown skin were the same in God's eyes.

It was Sadie who became a little prophet for us that day. She looked at all of us white people and said, "When a mama doggie has puppies, all the puppies have different colors and spots: there are white, brown, tan, and black ones. The mama dog loves all her puppies no matter what color they are. I guess that is how God sees us. God just loves us no matter what kind of skin we have. So, I'm going to love you. Won't you love me back?" I will always remember that teaching and prophetic moment. Later, I found a book about puppies and since have used it repeatedly as a resource for teaching God's love for everyone.

Two ingredients were necessary to get through to the heads and hearts of those six-year-old girls: first, the story about puppies, and second, our conversation about what that taught them about their behavior. It is stories, fables, and movies that can teach best in these situations. The animated film *Beauty and the Beast*, the story of *The Ugly Duckling*, among others, are great tools as we try to explain the power of acceptance and love of others.

KEEP TALKING

Finally, parents should not wait until there is a problem to talk to a child about prejudice. It is far better to start that conversation early in a child's life and keep it going. As parents we must be continually vigilant for opportunities to point out both good and bad examples of diversity and fairness. It is so much easier to allow God to orchestrate a teaching moment than to manufacture one. In the course of a child's everyday life examples will occur. We just need to connect the dots for the child. The best way to do this is with leading questions: "What do you think about Craig not being invited to Sam's party?" "How would you feel if you were excluded because of the color of your skin?" "Why do you think old people are ignored at the restaurant?"

It is also important to invite God into this process. We must pray for an end to prejudice and bigotry, pray for our children, and pray for all those we encounter each day. May we all understand the evil of separating the world family because of differences.

Remember

- Begin to teach your child justice by pointing out how and when to do what is fair.

- Be aware that your personal bias against any group or ideology will be inherited by your child. Know your silent resentments, personal biases, and prejudices.

- Talk with your child about society's unjust practices, using every example that comes into your daily life.

- Stop what you are doing at the very moment bigotry occurs and point it out to your child and clearly define it as grossly wrong.

- Start the conversation about bigotry, differences, and prejudices early in a child's life and keep it going.

- Invite God into this process. Pray for an end to prejudice and bigotry, pray for your child, and pray for all those you encounter each day.

Ponder

1. When did you stand up for what is right?

2. What prejudices or biases do you encounter?

3. When have you experienced the "we vs. they" syndrome?

4. In what ways do you or could you work for a change in justice for those who are being treated unfairly?

Exercise

Watch a movie about injustice with your family ("Beauty and the Beast," "The Rosa Parks Story," etc.). Talk about the issues in the film and how you as a family have encountered similar injustice and how you reacted to it.

Pray

O Divine Messiah, open my mind to my private moments of prejudice.

Fill my heart with compassion for those who are
victims of contempt.

Give me courage to speak up against the actions and
words of hate so that I may be the voice of your
love. Amen.

CHAPTER 9

Invite God

Only one more ingredient is necessary for raising a moral child: God.

We need to acknowledge and invite God into this process of forming moral children. When we surrender to God's power the lives of our children, a strange thing happens: everything is made stronger; everything prospers in ways beyond our expectations. I'm not saying this happens overnight. It is a *process* of coming into grace; it is a long journey of walking toward a goal when God walks with us.

Praying for our child releases a promise between God and parents. God promises to love, protect, and guide. We promise to teach our children the way of faith. In the Old Testament, this is called a "covenant," a solemn agreement to hold each other up. God tells us plainly that he will never forget his promises. We belong to God and so do our children. God loves them just like we do—only more.

I really never understood God's love until I held my firstborn baby girl in my arms for the first time. I looked at her and felt this enormous love that was deep within and far beyond me. It was God loving through me. It was and still is "divine." When we acknowledge that love and claim it for our children, we no longer are alone in the parent game. God joins us in each worry, each joy, each moment of pride. We cannot and should not try to parent alone. This is especially true for those of us who are single parents: we need to remember that God loves these children first and is next to us reaching out to keep our children safe and help them grow into men and women of faith.

The bluegrass musical group Old Crow Medicine Show sings a lyric that sustains me when I forget that God means to stay close: "We are all in this thing together, walking the line between faith and fear." Raising moral children is truly a time of walking the line between faith and fear. We want to believe in a God that cares for us, yet at the same time we are deathly afraid that God has forgotten us. What I must remind myself constantly is that even when I am scared for my child and worried sick about his or her welfare, I must believe in a God that will protect and keep both my child and me, just like a good shepherd keeps his sheep.

Inviting God into our parenting lives is simple. Some ways to do so which have worked for me and folks I know include:

PRAY THROUGH TOUGH DECISIONS

So many times in our relationship with our children, we are just not sure in which direction to turn: public school or private school; restrict time with a certain friend or allow the child to make his own decision about the friend; reward her for a job well done even though she did not succeed; and so on.

When I get stuck between my mother's heart and my teacher's head, I turn the matter over to prayer. I call it the "tomb method." I figure if Jesus could sit in the tomb for three days to think over the resurrection, I can mull over *my* decision for three days. During these three days I pray and ask others for advice and then, at the end of three days, I decide what to do, relying on God to lead me to the right outcome. Years of praying this way has led me to see that God does guide my thoughts and strengthen my confidence.

One of my sons is an excellent athlete. He was the typical high school jock who played sports all the time and studied rarely. He squeaked through high school and did poorly on his college entrance tests. When three "A" college teams offered scholarships and then rescinded them because of his grades, I knew my son was doomed. Seeing my discouragement, Sister Bertha, a fellow staff member, gave me a prayer to St. Joseph. She said that I should say it for nine days and St. Joseph would find my son a college. "Poppycock!" I told her. But I tried her advice just the same because I was desperate. After I said the prayer on the ninth day, the phone rang. It was the College of Mount St. Joseph with an offer for my son to go to college there and play sports.

I have prayed many times since then for my wild child. God kept his promise: my boy is a magna cum laude college graduate and a faith-filled husband and father. I believe prayer made all the difference.

HELP A CHILD TO DEVELOP DISCERNMENT AND CONSCIENCE

A life skill that is the key to finding what is the right thing to do can be a godsend to people of faith and those of us who are still working on it. Learning to discern what is right and to form a conscience is a lifelong process. It begins when we are very young. By age seven or eight, a child can distinguish the difference between a sin, an accident, and a mistake. It is at this point in a child's development that parents can lead the child through the process of discernment and forming a conscience. This skill is difficult as well for us grownups, so much patience with younger souls is needed.

First, we must state as plainly as we can what is our moral dilemma. It might be something like these dilemmas:

"I found ten dollars. Can I keep it?"

"I never get to play in a game. Can I quit the soccer team?"

"I heard my best friend lie to our teacher about home-work. Should I say anything to my friend or the teacher?"

Next, we must seek opinions and advice about the dilemma. If the situation is something we might read about in a resource like the *Catechism of the Catholic Church* or a text-book, we should go to that source. We also ask advice of three people whose opinions we respect.

Finally, we ask God to guide our decision. Then it is time to make up our minds. Slowly, we will begin to see a moral pattern emerge. Truth, good, and the moral right become more apparent as we experience this process of forming a conscience.

Children need our help in this process. It is important to look for opportunities when a moral dilemma arises and work with children in discerning the right thing to do.

Recently I was with two young brothers. Gus, the six-year-old older brother, had eaten all the pepperoni slices for his afternoon snack. His brother, Will, went to the refrigerator to get some pepperoni, and finding none, asked Gus where the pepperoni had gone. Gus told Will to keep looking: "It is in there somewhere." When Will said, "No, it's gone," Gus said, "I was just telling you a joke. I ate it all." As I overheard this conversation, I chimed in, "No, Gus, that was not a joke, it was a lie." I then used this opportunity to take Gus through the process I just outlined: What did you do that was wrong? What does God say about it? Why is lying wrong? Gus and I ended our chat by saying a short prayer about sharing snacks and being truthful. It was the six-year-old version of discernment.

LEARN TO SAY, "FORGIVE ME"

Have you ever known a person who cannot admit they made a mistake or did something wrong? These folks go through their lives convincing themselves that it is never their fault. Learning the humble art of saying "I'm sorry, please forgive me" is a real treasure. When we learn this, we are guaranteed that peace that Jesus promises.

Children truly respect their parent's actions. If a child never sees a parent, teacher, or coach admit they have failed, the child will grow up doing the same. Being honest with ourselves

and others can be painful, but without admitting we are not perfect, we cannot count on getting past the problem. Naming the
sin, problem, failure, mistake, or whatever frees us from its
bondage and opens the door to recovery. We must model forgiveness for our children, and it starts with telling them when
we have failed and asking for their forgiveness.

This is the most humbling thing a parent can do with a
child. We want our children to believe that we are perfect. But
we teach them a greater lesson when we teach them about forgiveness. The beauty of learning about forgiveness is that we
learn of God's unconditional love. God forgives us as we forgive
one another, the Lord's Prayer tells us. When we forgive one
another, parent to child, we are getting the message that true
love is unconditional. There is nothing we can do that will separate us from the love of God—nothing that will separate us
from each other's love. When we get that message, we understand that we are intrinsically lovable and failure is redeemable.
What a grace!

It is vital for parents to begin a personal challenge to admit
when we have failed and then to express our sorrow. This is a
difficult skill to learn in a secular world where failure makes us
vulnerable. In the end, we are doing ourselves a favor. Suddenly
we don't need to cover up our mistakes or make excuses. We
stand on the confidence that we are imperfect but working
toward perfection. When you are in a situation where you have
made a mistake, or failed your child, simply say, for example,
"Mommy is sorry she forgot to pick you up after band practice.
Forgive me." When we "walk the talk" about forgiveness, we
will raise a child who believes that there is always hope for a
new beginning.

PARTICIPATE IN THE SACRAMENT OF RECONCILIATION

If we want to take forgiveness up a notch, we go to confession. The sacrament of reconciliation has been one of the best kept secrets in the Catholic Church: it brings an inner peace that is beyond compare. In decades past, this ritual of forgiveness was all about making up for our sins. Once we figured out that God is not as interested in our attempts to do penance and is more concerned with mercy, we began to understand that every failure is redeemable. God literally yearns for us to come back to him with all our hearts.

That makes this sacrament a perfect place for our children to experience God's forgiveness and our forgiveness. The experience of speaking our sins to the priest (as the representative of God) and letting go of our pride in the process breeds strength and release from the bondage of regret and fear. All this sounds very theological, but the proof is in the experience. Trust the church to lead us into God's healing arms as we let go of that monkey on our backs.

When I prepare children for their first encounter with the sacrament of reconciliation, I worry that it will be difficult for them to understand and really experience God's love. I finally figured out that the children have little fear and seem very comfortable with sharing their weakness with God. They have been sharing those weaknesses with Mommy and Daddy since they were born. If we have been parents grounded in love and mercy, reconciliation is simply an affirmation of what children already know: God is a loving parent just like Mommy and Daddy.

Making the parish reconciliation service a part of a family's schedule is a good place to start to learn—as a family—to forgive and grow together. We parents need to get back in the habit of asking forgiveness of God as well. The extra benefit of the sacrament of reconciliation is that we experience this loving accountability in the naming of our failures. The kindness of the confessor's words reminds us that we are not in this alone. God cares and is ready to help us restore our lives, our relationships, and our peace of mind. I often wish I had some statistics to prove this to those who have not received this sacrament for years. All I can say is I have seen families healed, marriages renewed, and children freed of guilt because people have had the humility to ask for God's help.

PRAY AS A FAMILY

Morality needs an anchor and that anchor is prayer. Gathering as a family for meal prayers, night prayers, Sunday church, and spontaneous moments of connecting with the Divine One creates a foundation for the moral life. As soon as our little ones start talking to God, there is a desire to get to know God and what God asks of us. The conversation is life-long and is that anchor when we must choose to do the right thing. Knowing God guides us in being moral.

Lori was a bright little three-year-old when she offered to say the grace before meals at Grandma's house. "Thank you, God, for this food and for our friends. Mom will now help you with the snack. Amen." "Hmm," said Grandma, "I'll bet that is the prayer you say at nursery school." That was seven years ago. Today, both Lori, ten, and Grandma look forward to meal prayers that have evolved beyond that rote prayer. Lori asks God for help and Grandma often takes Lori's hand as they sense that God is with them and there is much gratitude for the food they will eat and for the intimacy they share that transcends the generations.

The God connection is the special ingredient that seals the deal for us parents. Prayer, forgiveness, and accountability to a higher power bring strength to the struggle of doing the right thing. We really are not alone: we have family, friends, and a merciful and loving God to help us raise a moral child and use our faith to help shape our child's behavior.

Remember

- Pray through tough decisions. Acknowledge and invite God to share with you in the process of forming a moral child.

- Help your child to develop discernment and conscience by stating the dilemma, seeking advice, and asking God to guide your and your child's decisions.

- Learn to say "forgive me" to your child. If your child never sees you or a teacher or coach admit a failure, your child will grow up never admitting his or her weakness.

- Participate in the sacrament of reconciliation as a family.

- Pray as a family when the going gets tough. Begin or end meals with a prayer. Bless your child as he or she heads for bed at night.

Ponder

1. Share a time when all you could do was pray for your child.

2. What are some moral dilemmas that children face? Is there a moral dilemma that your child faced?

3. Of whom would you like to ask forgiveness?

4. What excuses do you hear for why folks don't receive the sacrament of reconciliation? How could you counter these excuses?

Exercise

Gather a small wooden (or any unbreakable) bowl to use as a Prayer Bowl and then place a pen and small pieces of paper in or near the bowl. Keep this Prayer Bowl on a table or countertop where all in your family can find it. When someone needs prayer, write the person's name and prayer intention on the paper and place the paper in the bowl. Every night at meal prayer time, lift up the bowl and ask God to answer all the prayers collected in the bowl. Every so often empty the bowl of all those prayers that have been answered. With some intentions you may want to talk with your child about how prayers were answered.

Pray

Merciful God, hold me close to your heart.
Let me know that you forgive me

for whatever I have done that separates me from
    you.
Heal me from my pride,
and help me to let go of any anxiety or fear
which keeps me from accepting your mercy. Amen.